WORLD BANK WORKING PAPER NO. 52

The Regulation of Investment in Utilities

Concepts and Applications

Ian Alexander
Clive Harris

T0287667

THE WORLD BANK
Washington, D.C.

ISBN-10: 0-8213-6152-X   ISBN-13: 978-0-8213-6152-8
eISBN: 0-8213-6153-8   ISSN: 1726-5878

Ian Alexander is a Senior Economist in the South Asia Energy and Infrastructure unit of the World Bank. Clive Harris is a Lead Infrastructure Specialist in the South Asia Energy and Infrastructure unit of the World Bank.

Library of Congress Cataloging-in-Publication Data

Alexander, Ian, 1967
    The regulation of investment in utilities: concepts and applications/Ian Alexander, Clive Harris.
        p. cm.—(World Bank working paper, ISSn 1726-5878; no. 52)
        Includes bibliographical references.
        ISBN 0-8213-6152-X
        1. Public utilities—Great Britain—Finance. 2. Public utilities—Great Britain—Regulation. 3. Infrastructure (Economics)—Great Britain. I. Harris, Clive, 1965- II. Title. III. Series.

    HD2768.G74A44 2005
    332.67'22-dc22

                                                                    2005043154

Contents

Foreword v

Abstract vii

Acknowledgments ix

1. Introduction 1

2. Investment: Types and Characteristics 5
    Different Types of Investment 5
    Characteristics of Investment: Predictability and Controllability 6
    Assessing the Characteristics of the Different Types of Investment 7

3. Regulation and Investment: A framework. 9
    Determining Allowed Revenue. 9
    Inclusion of Assets in the Regulatory Asset Base 14
    Cost Allocation and Revenue Recovery Issues 20
    Case studies of the Regulatory Treatment of Investment. 21

4. Assessment of Investment Approaches 23
    Approaches to Inclusion of Assets in the Regulatory Asset Base. 24
    Assessment of Cost Allocation and Revenue Recovery Issues 34

5. Designing a Regulatory System to Handle Investment 41

Appendix: The Case Studies 49

Bibliography 139

LIST OF TABLES

2.1 Categorizing Investment in Airports 6
2.2 Summary on the Characteristics of Different Types of Investment 8
3.1 Main Approaches Presented in Case Studies 13
4.1 Risk Allocation of the Different Approaches 24
4.2 Illustrative NPV Impact of Logging-up 27
4.3 The Allocation of Risks and the Creation of Incentives—
     Lessons from the Case Studies 29
4.4 Compliance Costs 31
4.5 Summary on Compliance Costs 32
4.6 Ability to Handle Different Types of Investment 33

4.7   Risk Allocation of the Different Cost Allocation and Revenue Approaches 36
4.8   Ability to Handle Different Types of Investment 38

LIST OF CASE STUDIES

  1. Electricity and Water Transmission and Distribution in Abu Dhabi 50
  2. Argentina—Buenos Aires Water and Sewerage 55
  3. Argentine Electricity Transmission 59
  4. Electricity transmission in Australia 64
  5. Water and Sewerage in Chile 69
  6. Electricity Distribution, Chile 75
  7. Water and Sewerage Industry in England and Wales 79
  8. Electricity Transmission in England and Wales 96
  9. Gas Distribution in Great Britain 106
 10. Electricity Transmission and Generation in India 110
 11. Manila (Philippines) Water and Sewerage 117
 12. Electricity Transmission in Peru 120
 13. Water and Sewerage Industry in Scotland 125
 14. Electricity in Ukraine 129
 15. UK Airport Regulation 135

LIST OF FIGURES

3.1   The Elements of Allowed Revenue 10
3.2   Key Regulatory Issues Relating to Investment 14
3.3   Inclusion of Assets in the Regulatory Asset Base 15
3.4   Cost Allocation and Revenue Recovery Issues 20
4.1   Cash Flow Impact of Logging-up 27
4.2   Impact on Cash Flows of Different Variants of the ex-ante ex-post
       Approach and the Relative Impact of Accelerated Depreciation 28
4.3   The Impact of Choosing Different Degrees of Acceleration 37
5.1   Choosing an Approach to Inclusion of Investment 42
5.2   Determining Which Cost Allocation and Revenue Issues are Appropriate 44

LIST OF BOXES

3.1   Differential Rates of Return 11
3.2   Prudency: A Definition 16
3.3   The ACCC's Proposed Approach to Investment 17
3.4   Incentives for Investment Under the Model Company Approach 19
4.1   Dealing with Data Problems—Lessons from Abu Dhabi 34
5.1   Water and Sewerage in England and Wales—
       A Holistic Approach to Investment 42

Foreword

Regulatory institutions and the regimes that they establish have a significant impact on the environment for new investment in utility and infrastructure industries. This is especially true when the investment is provided by the private sector. A concern voiced around the world is that insufficient investment is being undertaken, and, consequently, regulators should take every effort to create an environment conducive to investment.

This paper reviews the common approaches adopted by regulators to the inclusion and valuation of investment in the regulatory asset base and the allocation of costs of investment between different users as well as between connection and usage charges. The former set of issues are key to the creation of incentives for companies to undertake efficient least-cost investment while the latter address the key concern of how revenues are recovered (and the associated risks for the operator). Understanding these issues, and how they relate to the investments that are needed in a sector, allows regulators an opportunity to better design regimes able to promote necessary investment.

Drawing on a worldwide series of case studies from across the regulated sectors, the paper illustrates the various approaches to regulating investment and some of the practical implementation problems that are faced. This allows some tentative suggestions for the design of practical investment regimes to be developed, depending upon the circumstances of the situation in hand.

Vincent Gouarne
Sector Director
South Asia Energy and Infrastructure Unit
The World Bank

Abstract

The last 15 years have seen a rapid growth in the number of specialized regulatory agencies in the infrastructure sectors. The success of these agencies in providing a framework conducive to investment is increasingly a focus in both developed and developing countries. Finance for a regulated utility will continue to be forthcoming if investors receive a return on this commensurate with the perceived risks. The sunk nature of much of utility investment means that investors are vulnerable to regulators changing the rules of the game after investment has been made. They will be less willing to provide funds if they are not confident of the broad rules of the game. The absence of this confidence has made some investors more wary of investing in developing-country infrastructure. However, efficiency in investment is critical from the consumers' viewpoint, as the capital intensity of many network utilities means that regulators, when giving incentives for investment, must avoid encouraging gold-plating and other inefficiencies.

In most situations, regulators have also felt the need to develop specific, and sometimes detailed, rules to deal with the way investment is incorporated into the setting of price controls. The treatment of investment is typically more complicated than, for example, ordinary maintenance costs. Some of this reflects uncertainty about the need for investments—unpredictability in demand, for example and legislative changes mandating investments to meet environmental targets. Investment may also receive more detailed scrutiny because in many situations the need for investment is very large—even on an ongoing basis because of the importance of fixed costs—but often at the initial stages of privatization because new investment may be high relative to written down asset values; and because of the lumpiness and indivisibility of many investments.

In response to this, regulators have developed a variety of approaches to dealing with investment decisions. This paper reviews the common approaches adopted by regulators to the inclusion and valuation of investment in the regulatory asset base and the allocation of costs of investment between different users as well as between connection and usage charges. The former set of issues are key to the creation of incentives for companies to undertake efficient least-cost investment while the latter address the key concern of how revenues are recovered (and the associated risks for the operator). By understanding these issues and how they relate to the investments that are needed in a sector, regulators have an opportunity to design regimes better able to promote necessary investment.

Drawing on a worldwide series of case studies from across the regulated sectors the paper illustrates the various approaches to regulating investment and some of the practical implementation problems that are faced. This allows some tentative suggestions for the design of practical investment regimes to be developed. The approach to be advocated will depend on the circumstances. For example, large predictable investments could be handled well through an ex-ante ex-post regime, possibly with positive or negative triggers linked to the delivery of the investment. However, a different approach might be required where investments are very unpredictable, in timing or volume. This means that it may be best for regulators to employ a portfolio of approaches which can deal with the different situations a utility faces. However, it will also be important to ensure that ensure that whatever portfolio is chosen is kept as simple as possible to limit compliance costs and minimize distortions to incentives for investment.

Acknowledgments

The authors would like to thank Katharina Gassner for her invaluable research work and the authors of the various case studies. The paper also benefited from comments provided by Chris Shugart, Timothy Irwin, David Kennedy, Aftab Raza, Eric Groom, Tony Ballance, Dejan Ostojic, Bernard W. Tenenbaum, and attendees at the London Business School workshop held in December 2003, as well as the participants at the Sixth SAFIR Core Course held in Pakistan in October 2004. This work, including the preparation of the case studies, was supported by the Infrastructure Economics and Finance Department of the World Bank.

Ian Alexander is a Senior Economist in the South Asia Energy and Infrastructure Unit and Clive Harris is a Lead Infrastructure Specialist in the South Asia Energy and Infrastructure Unit.

CHAPTER 1

Introduction

The last 15 years have seen a rapid growth in the number of specialized regulatory agencies in the infrastructure sectors. When dealing with natural monopolies, these agencies are typically charged with responsibilities that include ensuring that financing can be attracted to the sector, providing incentives to promote efficiency, and, very often, promoting equity—for example, access by particular groups of consumers to regulated services. Fulfilling these responsibilities requires protecting the interests of consumers and ensuring that the regulated utilities invest sufficiently to expand output and maintain quality levels.

The success of these agencies in providing a framework conducive to investment is increasingly a focus in both developed and developing countries. In the UK, where the goal of RPI-X regulation during the 1990s was to provide incentives for reducing costs, concerns about incentives for investment were highlighted in the National Audit Office "Pipes and Wires" report (NAO 2002).[1] The need for new infrastructure investments in developing countries is vast. In the power sector alone, the IEA (2003) has estimated that to keep pace with growing demand, developing countries will have to invest annually around $120 billion over the period 2001–2010. During the 1990s, private capital flows made a substantial contribution to meeting these needs in some countries. Private flows have fallen considerably in recent years. From a peak of $50 billion in 1997, investment in power projects with private participation in developing countries fell to around $14 billion in 2003.[2]

---

1. See, for example, Part 3: Regulators are seeking to address the risks arising from price cap regulation.
2. World Bank PPI Database. Note, this figure includes both the payment for existing assets as well as commitments for new investment. Available at http://ppi.worldbank.org.

Finance for a regulated utility will continue to be forthcoming if investors receive a return on this commensurate with the perceived risks. The sunk nature of much of utility investment means that investors are vulnerable to regulators changing the rules of the game after investment has been made.[3] They will be less willing to provide funds if they are not confident of the broad rules of the game. The absence of this confidence has made some investors more wary of investing in developing country infrastructure.[4] To address this there have been calls for greater specificity of the parameters and approaches to be used in regulation, including setting this out in contractually binding documents.[5] From the consumers' viewpoint, the capital intensity of many network utilities means that while giving incentives for investment regulators must not encourage gold-plating and inefficiencies in investment.

The approach taken to the broad parameters—operating costs, depreciation and the return on the financing provided by investors represent critical rules of the game. Incentives for investment are strongly influenced by whether the cost of capital allowed by the regulator closely approximates the investor's perceived cost of capital; whether the operating costs allowed reflect realistic estimates of what can be achieved by the utility; and whether the regulator has a clear approach to the valuation of assets already in place. The overall structure of the price control also provides incentives, for example price caps provide an incentive to expand output beyond the level forecast at the price determination, as opposed to revenue caps that do not.

In most situations, regulators have also felt the need to develop specific, and sometimes detailed, rules governing how they treat investments when setting price controls. The treatment of investment has typically been more complicated than, for example, ordinary maintenance costs. Some of this reflects uncertainty about the need for investments—unpredictability in demand, for example and legislative changes mandating investments to meet environmental targets. However, uncertainty affects all inputs. Investment may receive more detailed scrutiny because in many situations the need for investment is very large—even on an ongoing basis because of the importance of fixed costs—even more so at the initial stages after privatization because new investments may be high relative to written down asset values; and because of the lumpiness and indivisibility of many investments.

In response to this, regulators have developed a variety of approaches to dealing with investment decisions. These differ in the extent to which forecast or actual levels of investment are used, the degree of scrutiny of investment decisions, the way changes in factors driving investment are incorporated, and the way investments are recovered. This paper provides a broad assessment of these different approaches. The goal of the paper is to provide a broad framework for assessing alternative regulatory regimes towards investment, providing an overview of the different approaches as applied in practice, and an assessment of situations that might favor one particular approach as opposed to another.

---

3. See Levy and Spiller (1997), among others for a discussion of this issue. The recent focus of Ofcom in the UK on this issue is discussed in Williamson (2004).

4. The results of this survey are reported in Lamech and Saeed (2003).

5. See for example Bakovic, Tenenbaum and Woolf (2003).

The structure of the paper is as follows:

- Chapter 2 provides an overview of the investment problem facing utilities, looking at different types of investment and their characteristics;
- Chapter 3 provides an overall framework for the regulation of investment, and describe some of the main approaches used by regulators towards investment;
- Chapter 4 provides an assessment of these different approaches based on specific criteria, namely their ability to handle different types of investment; the incentives they provide; and the likely cost of the regulatory process. This is complemented by some financial modeling of these approaches;
- Chapter 5 concludes by drawing out lessons and recommendations for the design of regulatory systems to address investment; and
- The Appendix presents a set of short case studies of how regulators in different countries and sectors have developed mechanisms to deal with investment.

CHAPTER 2

Investment: Types and Characteristics

Two important factors considered by regulators in developing approaches to dealing with investment concern the extent to which individual investments can be forecast with confidence, and the extent to which they are under the control of the utility. To some extent this depends on the nature of the investment involved. This chapter therefore looks at the main forms of investment and their characteristics, in particular in relation to the two factors—predictability and controllability—mentioned above.

Different Types of Investment

Investment can be directed either at:

- *Replacement investment*, where existing assets are repaired to ensure continued provision of an existing service at present quality levels, given the continual consumption of capital inputs during their use; or
- *New investment*, where new assets are provided to improve quality or expand output, or both. New investments aimed at expanding quality may be addressing issues such as reliability and the quality of the service *per se*, or the mitigation of environmental impacts that arise from producing the service.

The relative importance of each type of investment will depend on the circumstances. In countries with low connection rates for electricity and water the priority may be expansion of the service. Countries with higher connection rates but significant technical and commercial losses may rank the rehabilitation of existing assets as a higher priority. One estimate has found that, for low- and middle-income developing countries, expected

Table 2.1 Categorizing Investment in Airports

Example of investment	Type of investment
Y2K compliance	Mainly aimed at ensuring continued levels of past capacity and quality.
Runway overlay	Either replacement or new investment, depending on the extent to which the overlay will increase capacity, *e.g.* by strengthening the runway and allowing heavier and larger aircraft.
New runway	New investment.
Capitalization of O&M through an investment	Most likely replacement as no clear expansion of output or improvement of quality.
New fittings in terminal	New if there has been a net enhancement of service.

Source: ACCC 2000.

annual infrastructure investments will see a roughly 50–50 split between new and replacement investments, whereas for high-income developing countries replacement investment will account for two thirds of the total (Fay and Yepes 2003).

Although it is possible to draw a conceptual distinction between new and replacement investment, actual investments often serve both purposes, because of indivisibilities and economies of scale. For example, when rehabilitating electricity transmission and distribution lines it is normal for some expansion work to be undertaken at the same time, increasing the capacity of the system. Deciding whether or not a particular investment improves quality or expands output, or simply maintains services at existing levels, may require some analysis. Table 2.1 provides some hypothetical examples quoted by the Australian Competition and Consumer Commission (ACCC 2000) on what might constitute new or replacement investment in airports.

Regulatory regimes may provide different incentives for expanding output as opposed to improving the quality of service. While additional sales of, say, electricity, generate additional revenue since units of electricity are priced, this might not be the case with improvements in quality. Relatively few regulatory regimes explicitly price quality, although many will include penalties that are levied if certain service quality measures fall below agreed standards.[6]

Characteristics of Investment: Predictability and Controllability

The factors that drive the need for a specific investment, and the cost of this, may be difficult to predict and out of the hands of the utility. It is important therefore, in considering different types of investment, to examine:

> ▓ *predictability*—the ease with which the need for that type of investment can be forecast; and

6. See NAO (2002) and Burns and Reichmann (2004) for more information on incentives for making investment in improving quality.

▓ *controllability*—the extent to which the utility can control expenditure on this investment, which in turn can be split into:

    ● *volume*—how much control over the volume of investment needed does the company exert? And

    ● *unit cost*—can the company control the unit cost of the investment?

Very often it is difficult for companies to predict the amount and cost of investment required several years ahead. Forces outside of the sector often drive the levels of investment required. For example, the vast majority of the £50 billion of investment undertaken in the water and sewerage industry in England and Wales over the 15 years since privatization in 1989 was mandated by the European Union, rather than the sector regulator, to meet environmental objectives.

Assessing the Characteristics of the Different Types of Investment

Whether the need for an individual investment can be predicted with much certainty, or whether the company concerned can influence much control over the costs of this investment will depend on the precise circumstances. However, it is possible to make assessments in general about the predictability and controllability of the different types of investments noted above.

First we consider predictability. *Replacement investment* should in general not be too difficult to predict since the company should have knowledge of the state of the assets, and the need for rehabilitation. However, in some situations, for example newly privatized utilities with poor information on assets and demand, it is likely to be much harder to predict required levels of replacement investment. Utilities that have much of their assets underground may also find it harder to predict replacement investment needs, particularly when maintenance and inspection of assets in the past was inadequate.

Quality enhancements can come from two main sources: either mandated or incentivized by the sector regulator as part of a pre-arranged program or driven by factors outside the sector, for example a national environmental agency. Quality enhancement mandated within the sector is likely to be more predictable than that mandated by external forces.

As far as *expansion* investment is concerned, the extent to which this can be predicted with confidence depends on the circumstances. Out-turn demand may well differ substantially from what is forecast and some driving factors may be inherently harder to predict. For example, in electricity transmission it is likely that the transmission company will have several years notice of the need to connect new generating plant to the system. But some major new customers could occur with little notice, or at least less notice than that needed to build the investment into the typical four to five year duration of a price control.

Next, consider controllability. *Replacement investment* often lends itself to flexibility in terms of timing—it should be possible to move the timing forwards and backwards as necessary, and therefore the volume of replacement should be to a considerable extent controllable by the utility. The unit costs of investment may well not be, however. *Quality investment* is largely outside the control of the utility. Either the sector regulator or other agencies set the parameters which drive quality standards, and the utility has limited scope

Table 2.2 Summary on the Characteristics of Different Types of Investment

	Predictability	Controllability	
		Volume	Cost
Maintenance and rehabilitation	High	High	Mixed
Quality improvement	Mixed	Low	Low
System expansion	Mixed	Low	Mixed

to influence the volume of this and often the unit costs, since this may depend on the quality parameter being targeted.

The situation is also complicated for *expansion investment*. Taking the example of power transmission in a vertically separated system, the decisions on how much new generation capacity will be added, where it will be located, and where generating capacity will be closed are not taken by the transmission utility. Out-turn investment may therefore be different from forecast because of differences in the volume and location of generation, for example, and not be the result of any efficiency of inefficiency on the part of the transmission utility. It is also worth noting that the utility may have a number of options it can pursue to meet the increases in demand—for example it might be possible to contract for demand management or local generation to defer network investments.

It should also be recognized that the timing of construction of assets may rely on the decisions of others. Thus, even where the need for the construction of a particular asset may be known, where this relies on planning consent and other authorizations provided by local governments and other agencies, the timing may to some extent be outside the control of the utility.

Across all three types of investment, the utility probably has some control over the costs for an investment plan of a given size, to the extent that it can alter solutions required to meet the objectives. This assessment is summarized in Table 2.2.

The lumpiness of many, though not all, infrastructure investments means that in some cases uncertainty about timing can have major impacts. For example, the cost of Terminal 5 at Heathrow Airport in the UK is estimated to be around 25 percent of the existing value of the company undertaking this, the British Airports Authority (BAA). Taking into account these considerations alongside controllability and predictability will help assess the magnitude of the risks that are being faced by the utility.

CHAPTER 3

Regulation and Investment: A Framework

The overall regulatory framework within which the company operates plays a large role in determining the incentives for investment. This includes the return on capital that regulators allow, the treatment of depreciation, and the incentives for efficiency provided for both operations and maintenance costs and investment. In this chapter we provide a brief overview of the typical approaches taken by regulators to setting prices and some of the broader issues that arise. We then review some of the main approaches taken to dealing with investment, and particularly how they try to address issues of controllability and predictability. Finally, we describe in brief the set of case studies presented in the Appendix, focusing on the techniques used by regulators and the issues they are seeking to address in developing and implementing these techniques.

Determining Allowed Revenue

The main elements in the revenue calculation undertaken in a typical price control are set out in Figure 3.1.[7]

Allowance for Operating Costs

Operating and maintenance costs reflect the fixed and variable costs associated with the actual provision of the service—for example, labor, fuel, and other inputs, spares, and so forth. Some of these costs are under the control of the company and others are externally

---

7. Green and Pardina (1999) provides a detailed review of the way in which the Argentine gas regulator undertook its first price review and an overall description of setting price controls.

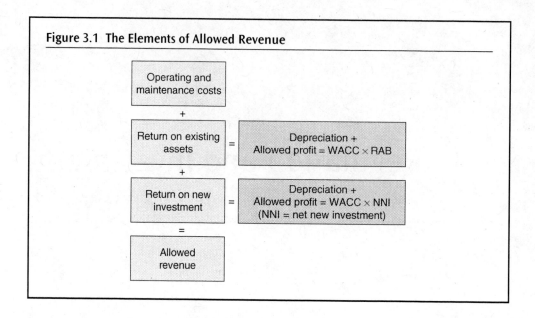

Figure 3.1 The Elements of Allowed Revenue

driven and consequently treated as cost pass-through items. Costs held to be under the control of the company will typically be benchmarked and de-linked to some extent from the actual figures for the company to provide incentives for efficiency. The time period over which companies are allowed to keep efficiency savings is an important factor in determining their incentives to reduce these costs. Costs outside the control of the utility will typically be subject to pass-through.[8]

Remuneration of Capital Invested

Investors must be remunerated for the capital employed in the provision of the service, both for existing capital and for additions to the capital stock (net new investment). This occurs through two separate charges:

- the opportunity cost of the capital employed which is proxied by the allowed rate of return, which reflects the cost of both debt and equity finance; and
- the consumption of the existing asset to provide the service, proxied by the depreciation charge.

It is important for the regulator to get the estimate of the allowed rate of return as close to the actual cost of capital. If the rate of return allowed is above the cost of capital, then every dollar invested will make the operator profits.[9] An allowed rate of return above the cost of capital will give companies an incentive to overinvest (Averch and Johnson 1962). If the rate of return is less than the cost of capital, the operator will be earning less than it needs

---

8. For a description of the issue of controllability see Alexander and Harris (2001).
9. Here profits are being considered in the economic sense, not the accounting. 'Normal' profit, or the cost of capital is considered as a cost by economists. So in this case, supernormal profits are being earned.

Box 3.1 Differential Rates of Return

Should new investments be allowed a higher rate of return than the average for the company? Several regulators have addressed this issue and proposed different solutions.

When Terminal 5 (T5) at Heathrow Airport was being reviewed at the last price determination the regulator, the Civil Aviation Authority (CAA) proposed that the project should be handled separately and a higher rate of return allowed. They were suggesting that T5 had a higher beta value as well as a higher debt premium than the rest of the airport operator and so an allowed rate of return of 8.5% rather than the 7 to 7.5% proposed for the rest of the operator.

The Competition Commission which is also responsible for reviewing airport pricing decisions suggested a different approach. Rather than keeping T5 separate they wanted to increase the overall allowed rate of return—they had proposed a rate of 7.2% for the existing assets. An increase of about 0.3% was proposed for T5 risks which included:

- the operator having to undertake the project at an earlier date than would occur in a competitive market and a consequent loss of the real option value of delaying;
- the revenue risks introduced by the triggers (discussed in Chapter 4 of this report); and
- the overall impact on gearing which would increase the debt premium and the cost of equity.

Given these T5 risks plus some other concerns the overall allowed rate of return was increased to 7.75%.

Another example of new investments being allowed a higher rate of return is seen in the US. FERC proposed a transmission pricing policy that provides a 100 basis point (1%) bonus on the Return on Equity for transmission investments that strengthen grid performance in Regional Transmission Organizations.

Sources: A report on the economic regulation of the London Airports companies (Heathrow Airport Ltd, Gatwick Airport Ltd and Stansted Airport Ltd), Competition Commission, 2002.
Proposed Pricing Policy for Efficient Operation and Expansion of Transmission Grid, FERC, 2003.

to remunerate investors.[10] Many regulators are concerned that the costs of setting the allowed cost of capital too low—underinvestment—are more serious than the possible overinvestment generated by setting the allowed cost of capital too high. The perceived asymmetry in outcomes may lead some to avoid setting this critical parameter too low.

The estimation of the allowed rate of return is one of the time-consuming and important issues facing regulators. The main approaches to setting the cost of capital, and general methodologies towards determining the regulatory asset base, are well covered in a number of sources and readers are referred to these to understand the methodology and data requirements.[11] All regulators face data limitations in trying to determine this estimate, but this may be particularly an issue for those operating in developing countries without well-developed financial markets. Options for handling some of the data issues are provided in Alexander and Estache (1997).[12]

In some situations regulators have allowed differential rates of return on either new investment, or particular types of investment, as outlined in Box 3.1. Regulators may also

---

10. It is assumed that there are no efficiency savings possible and all that is earned is that which the regulator is allowing.

11. See for example Green and Pardina (1999), Alexander (1995) and Foster and Antmann (2004).

12. Case studies considering how different regulators have actually dealt with this problem as well as a longer discussion on the issues of data availability are addressed in Alexander (forthcoming).

allow accelerated depreciation—effectively allowing higher capital charges—where the term of loans used to finance assets is considerably less than the life of the asset. This approach has been used by some regulators in the power sector in India (see the Appendix and Table 3.1).

Incentives for Efficiency and Gaming

Price controls are typically set for a medium-term period—for example, around four to five years, to provide incentives for efficiency gains, as firms retain the profits gained by reducing controllable costs below levels anticipated by the regulator. These gains will at some point be returned to consumers through allowed costs lower than they would have been without the additional efficiency savings, and hence lower prices. The distribution of these efficiency gains between investors and consumers will depend on how quickly regulators adjust their estimates of allowed costs. An immediate adjustment at the start of the next price control provides consumers with the benefits earlier. A glide-path adjusting allowed costs gradually would give more of the benefits to the company. There is some evidence that companies, either uncertain about the pace of adjustment or anticipating a rapid return of efficiency gains to consumers, delay efficiency gains in the years at the end of one price control and into the first years of the next price control.[13]

Efficiency savings may apply both to investment and to operating costs. If a company finds that it can meet demand with a lower investment than anticipated, then it should keep some of these gains. However, this raises issues about the extent to which gaming by the company might arise. One possible source of gaming would be overestimating demand and therefore the required investment plan. Another source might be to forecast that capital investments might be needed early in the period, with prices adjusted to allow for this, then delay it to later years in the price control period. In some situations regulators might want to have recourse to an ex-post adjustment mechanism to return some of the benefits associated with mis-estimation or gaming to consumers. However, the challenge will be to distinguish between this and the genuine efficiency gains made by companies.[14]

A second source of gaming might arise from the extent to which regulators use benchmarks or estimates of the company's own costs in the calculation of the price control. Incentives for reducing controllable costs—whether operating or related to investment—are provided by some form of benchmarking, substituting the costs of an efficient company, or industry best practice, for the company's own costs. If some costs are set on a benchmark basis and some on the basis of pass-through of the company's own costs, there will be incentives for the company to transfer costs from the benchmarked to the non-benchmarked costs. There have been some arguments that regulators typically benchmark operating costs more thoroughly than investment, with some incentives for the capitalization of operating costs through investment (NAO 2002; Burns and Reichmann 2004).

---

13. See for example NAO (2002).

14. See Alexander and Shugart (1999) for a more detailed analysis of the extent to which different broad regulatory regimes provide incentives for gaming by companies.

Table 3.1 Main Approaches Presented in Case Studies

Country and sectors	Ex-ante ex-post (3.2.1)	Ex-post : Logging-up (3.3.2)	Ex-post (3.3.2)	Interim determination (3.2.3)	Error Correction/Volume Flexibility (3.2.4)	Contracting-out (3.2.5)	Model Firm (See 3.2.2)	Revenue triggers (see 3.2.1)	Connection charging (3.3.1)	Deep/shallow pricing (3.3.2)	Accelerated Depreciation (see 3.1)	Replacement Expenditure (3.3.3)	Pre-payment (3.3.4)
Abu Dhabi: electricity and water distribution and transmission		×											
Argentina: Buenos Aires water and sewerage	×	×				×			×				
Argentina: electricity transmission													
Australia: electricity transmission	×	×											
Chile: water and sewerage							×						
Chile: electricity distribution							×						
England & Wales: water and sewerage	×	×							×	×			
England & Wales: electricity transmission				×									
Great Britain: gas distribution	×				×								
India: electricity transmission			×	×	×						×	×	×
Philippines: water and sewerage	×	×										×	×
Peru: electricity transmission			×			×	×						
Scotland: water and sanitation						×							
Ukraine: electricity			×										
United Kingdom: airports								×				×	×

This might lead to suboptimal investments and gold-plating, even where the return is below the allowed cost-of-capital.

Approaches Toward the Treatment of Investment

Investment—in existing and new assets—is a major issue for regulators in the development of price controls. Issues surrounding controllability and predictability are important for all items in the cost function of a utility, but the nature of capital investments in utilities—their size, lumpiness and indivisibility—have prompted regulators to develop specific approaches to dealing with the controllability and predictability of investment. We focus here on the specific ways in which regulators approach investment for the purposes of setting price controls, which can be divided broadly into two areas:

▦ whether or not assets are included in the regulatory asset base (RAB), and the value assigned to these assets for the purposes of inclusion in the RAB; and
▦ the allocation of costs associated with these investments, including charging for different outputs provided (connections and access, and quality), and whether revenues are raised from present or future consumption.

In the remainder of Chapter 3 we outline some of the main approaches to addressing the details of these three main areas. We do not present general approaches to determining whether demand justifies investment in an asset, estimating the cost of assets or investments, nor to setting price control mechanisms, which are all well described in other sources. Here we focus on those issues which are specific to dealing with the predictability and controllability issues as relating to investment.

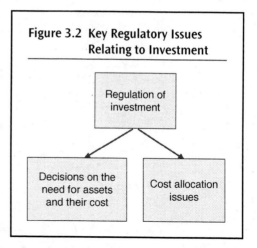

Figure 3.2 **Key Regulatory Issues Relating to Investment**

Inclusion of Assets in the Regulatory Asset Base

Most regulatory approaches will develop an *ex-ante* assessment of the amount of investment at the start of a price control period, and include in the price control an allowance for the costs associated with this. There is often then an *ex-post* review, at the end of the price control period, which may result in some adjustments made to the level of investment actually included in the RAB, as well as other adjustments.

Different approaches to the inclusion of assets in the RAB use these forward and backward looking approaches to varying degrees. In some situations, regulators have only adopted "ex-post" approaches, with no upfront inclusion of investment. Below we characterize five main approaches to the inclusion of assets in the RAB, as set out in Figure 3.3. In practice, regulators have combined different approaches to address the full range of issues associated with investment programs.

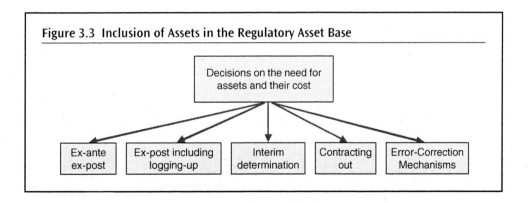

Figure 3.3 Inclusion of Assets in the Regulatory Asset Base

Decisions on the need for assets and their cost

| Ex-ante ex-post | Ex-post including logging-up | Interim determination | Contracting out | Error-Correction Mechanisms |

Ex-ante/ex-post

As described above, this approach involves an estimate of the needed investment being made at the time of the price determination (the *ex-ante* aspect) and incorporated into the RAB, so allowing a return on the investment and depreciation to be earned. At the next price determination an *ex-post* review occurs. This typically has the *ex-ante* investment figures that were incorporated into the RAB replaced with the out-turn figures. This approach is used in most of the regulated UK industries, the Manila water concessions and most of the regulated Australian industries.

Several implementation issues arise with this approach. The first is the timing of the switch from *ex-ante* to *ex-post* figures. Different options used by regulators for switching include:

- at the next price control determination and so the incentive exists for a maximum of five years and a minimum of one year—depending on when within the price control period the investment is actually undertaken;
- at the second price control determination after the investment occurs and so the incentive exists for a maximum of 10 years and a minimum of six; and
- on a rolling basis so that there is always a five year incentive, no matter when during a price control period the investment is actually undertaken.

As part of this, regulators also have to address whether, in the event of overspend, the utility is allowed to recover nothing during the price control period, just depreciation, or the full return on this investment.

A second set of issues arise in the intrusiveness and scope of the *ex-post* review. Regulators might try to investigate the prudency of investment decisions at the time they were made. The concept of "used and useful," as used in US regulatory practice, has evolved to focus on the current utilization of the assets rather than whether the decision to invest in the assets was appropriate for the circumstances faced at the time of the investment decision. Box 3.2 provides an example of an approach to defining prudency. However, regulators may also try to go further than this, and try to assess, *ex-post*, the outcome of the investment. This issue is addressed further in Chapter 4 where demand and obsolescence risk is considered.

This sort of assessment can introduce additional risks for the utility and introduce asymmetries into the ways in which certain factors, such as demand risks, are addressed.

Box 3.2 Prudency: A Definition

An issue that has exercised the Independent Pricing and Regulatory Tribunal (IPART) in New South Wales, Australia—the regulatory body for the utility and infrastructure companies in that State—was what prudency actually means. Over the past few years IPART has provided information on how it would define prudency through a series of letters, decisions and pieces of consultancy work. In 2001 through a letter, IPART clarified that when thinking about prudency it would expect investment decisions to be consistent with good industry practice, including:

- current and projected capacity;
- current condition of assets and renewal requirements;
- alternatives of contracting for support through demand management and distributed generation (taking into account emerging trends in technology and costs);
- current safety standards for the distribution network and accepted planning standards;
- current and foreseeable policies in regard to factors such as environmental requirements and contestability;
- current demand and reasonable projections for demand; and
- analysis of the risks attached to the above elements.

Terms of reference for consultancy support on operating and capital expenditure issues published in 2002 provided further clarification. A clear standard definition of prudency was provided but this was then interpreted for the price control process. What was made clear was that hindsight should not have an impact—an investment decision's prudency should be based on the information that was available when the decision was taken, not at the time of the review.

Sources: 1. Letter to CEO's of the distribution companies: *Tribunal Guidance on Prudency Test for Capital Expenditure by Electricity Distributors*, IPART, 2001.
2. Invitation to tender: *Review of Capital Expenditure and Operating Expenditure of the NSW Distribution Network Service Providers*, IPART, 2002.

For example, if demand is lower than anticipated, an asset may be underutilized, and the regulator might be tempted to disqualify some of the costs associated with this as a result. However, if demand is above what was anticipated, the regulator would presumably assess the investment as needed but cap return at the allowed cost of capital. A review of the decision to invest would not lead to such asymmetries in treatment (Concho and McKenzie 2004).

Regulators in the UK are increasingly trying to address the issue of dealing with overruns in investment programs. The energy regulator, OFGEM, has recently set out its approach to assessing overspend, which would include tests to determine whether or not the spending was wasteful, efficient or not, and whether consumers have significantly benefited from such investments. Depending on whether or not an investment passes one or both of these tests, the amount earned on it may vary from nothing at all (if deemed to be "wasteful"), nothing but depreciation and return at the next price control period, or some depreciation during the present period and return plus depreciation subsequently (if deemed "efficient"), to full recovery from the year of spend if deemed to be efficient and in consumers' interests. It remains to be seen how the tests for these will be elaborated in practice.

Box 3.3 The ACCC's Proposed Approach to Investment

The ACCC intends to shift from a backward-looking ex-post prudency test to a forward-looking firm ex-ante cap approach when regulating energy markets. Under this new approach, an assessment of investment needs will be made at the start of the price control period, and incorporated into estimated required price levels. At the end of the price control period, the ACCC will roll into the asset base the lesser of the actual investment or the estimate made at the start of the price control. It will not engage in a detailed assessment of the individual investments made as part of the ex-post review. Any expenditure above the cap level will require additional justification.

Source: Willet 2004.

A Simplified ex-ante Approach?

The *ex-post* review of investment leaves utilities vulnerable to the disqualification or reduction in allowed expenditures, and the stranding of assets, where assets are written-out or the value is written down for whatever reason (lack of use, technological change etc.).[15] This can substantially increase the regulatory risk faced by utilities. Arguably, there has also been a tendency for *ex-post* scrutiny to become increasingly detailed and intrusive. Some regulators are considering changes to these approaches to reduce regulatory risks and to simplify approaches to this review by doing away with the scrutiny of individual investments under a program (see Box 3.3). Such an approach would however still have to develop a satisfactory way of dealing with overspend.

Triggers

As noted above, one of the concerns regulators clearly have with building in ex-ante projections of investments is what to do if the investment is not undertaken within the time frame. This may particularly be a problem if the investment is large relative to existing assets. While an ex-post review might provide an opportunity for correction, some regulators have also developed incentives or penalties relating to investments by establishing trigger values that are used within the period of a given price control. An incentive would be created if greater revenue is allowed as investments become operational (say by adjusting the X value) and a penalty would exist if revenue is reduced if a company fails to deliver investments on time. A penalty-based approach has been adopted by the UK airports regulator—described in Case Study 15 in the Appendix—while an example of a positive trigger can be found in the Argentine gas sector.

Ex-post

Pure *ex-post* approaches do not undertake an upfront forecast of the level of investment required during the price control period. Prices set at the start of the price control do not therefore include an allowance for investment. Instead, all assessment occurs at the end of the price control period during the determination of the next price control. This type of approach has also been used in the power sector in India, Peru and the Ukraine.

---

15. See Sidak and Spulber (1998) for a review of this issue.

A second *ex-post* approach, *logging-up* (and logging-down) involves more formalized and specific rules that govern how and when *ex-post* reviews will take place. Sometimes these logging-up approaches also include considerable detail on the treatment of carrying costs (financing costs), the need for reviews of the investments to be included and what types of costs/investments may be eligible for logging-up. In some cases this is done for the entire investment program, as was the practice in Abu Dhabi when independent regulation was first introduced. In other cases it is used only for specific circumstances, and to supplement other approaches to the regulation of investment, for example in water and sewerage in Manila where logging-up is used in conjunction with *ex-ante* and *ex-post* approaches.

Important issues that occur in all *ex-post* reviews and have to be addressed are the extent to which carrying-costs—or financing costs—of investments logged-up are allowed for, as well as the extent to which the concerned assets are depreciated when included in the RAB at the next price determination.[16]

The Model Firm

From this standpoint, the model firm approach is somewhat akin to a radical ex-post review, not just of investment and the asset base but also of other inputs. It differs from other approaches presented here inasmuch as the basic philosophy is one focused on a hypothetical company facing an idealized world rather than some form of the actual company.[17] When using the model company approach a regulator is basically:

- establishing the characteristics of an optimal or efficient firm for the situation faced by the existing operator at that time (or over a forward looking period);
- determining the price that the optimal company would charge with this efficient set of assets and operating practices; and
- allowing the company to take decisions as to how to deliver the required outputs given the allowed price.

Box 3.4 considers the incentives for investment created under the model company approach, particularly focusing on how it has been applied in practice.

Interim Determinations

An interim determination is a process by which the regulator is requested to review the investment and determine a new price control (or incremental control) for the company.[18] Several options exist for the design of an interim determination system:

- asymmetric—company only allowed to request;
- symmetric—both company and regulator can request;

---

16. In the case of the water and sewerage industry in England and Wales it is interesting to note that no allowance for carrying-costs is made and consequently companies are incentivized to minimize investment that is subject to logging-up (or to maximize it so that an interim determination is brought about). It should also be noted that the vast majority of investment in this sector falls under the *ex-ante ex-post* approach—for example, less than 10 percent was captured through logging-up between 1994 and 1999.

17. Two of the case studies, both from Chile, investigate the model company approach.

18. Interim determinations can also address changes in operating costs.

Box 3.4 Incentives for Investment Under the Model Company Approach

---

Under the standard approach the optimal company is chosen at a specific point in time and reflecting the characteristics of that situation (demand, external costs, and so forth)—some regulators try to make this more dynamic by considering expected demand growth etc over the life of the price control period. This establishes a price that reflects the optimal situation and which normally will be below the revenue required by the operator to be profitable—since there are economies of scale in most infrastructure businesses. There are also likely to be previously determined investments that are now determined to be inappropriate and so stranded, consequently imposing a cost on the operator.

In this situation, incentives for investment are introduced through additional measures. Firstly, it is often the case that there are adjustments made to tariffs set on a model company basis to provide for some level of minimum return. It is also the case that service standards, for example relating to quality of service for consumers, will lead to penalties if they are not met and a loss of revenue, providing incentives to invest to maintain these standards.

- event or impact specific—the elements that can trigger an interim determination may be closely defined or left open, also whether a materiality test is needed to determine whether an interim determination is appropriate must be determined; and
- investment specific or company wide—does the interim determination just consider the costs associated with the investment or does it become a full price review considering the efficiency savings made, other costs etc.

Several of the case studies have interim determinations, most with materiality thresholds, such as those in Chile. When unexpected but significant expenditures can occur, such as with environmentally driven investments in the water industry, significant utilization of the approach can be expected, as seen in the water and sewerage sectors in England and Wales.

Error-Correction Mechanisms and Volume Adjustments

When faced with uncertain levels of investment, for example caused by uncertain estimates of demand, regulators have tried to develop mechanistic formulas for updating RABs for the purposes of setting price controls. One example is the approach adopted by OFGEM in the UK regarding the price control for the National Grid Company (NGC). Here, the regulator allowed an automatic adjustment in the RAB of £23 mn for every 1GW of new connected generating capacity above or below forecast levels. This approach was adopted because NGC had little control over the pace of new connections but it was felt possible to forecast the average cost of connecting 1 GW of capacity.[19] Although the example has some desirable characteristics for handling uncertainties associated with investment, the actual implementation was less successful owing to the variability of actual connection charges—especially related to smaller renewables-based generation.

---

19. See Case Study 8 in the Appendix on electricity transmission in England and Wales.

Contracting-out

An alternative approach to delivering investments is for the operator to pass responsibility for the cost and delivery of an investment to a third party, through contracting-out. If that third party is chosen through a competitive process then the cost of the investment would be whatever the competition establishes. Instead of attempting to assess the cost of the investment, the regulator would instead be concerned with the selection of appropriate investment projects and ensuring that a competitive procurement process is properly implemented. In some cases, for example where investment schemes are contracted out to a third part under a BOT scheme, this may lead to what would have been a capital charge for investment being converted into an operating charge.

Cost Allocation and Revenue Recovery Issues

The design of the pricing system and what is included is an important element of the regulatory treatment of investment and can have a significant impact on the incentives for investment and the risk allocation. This includes the extent to which investment costs are recovered from specific users or all users (deep versus shallow pricing), explicitly linking quality of service to revenues recovered from consumers, and the extent to which revenues remunerating investments are recovered from existing consumers rather than future ones.

Connection Charging

Connection to a system is often paid-for by the user being connected and consequently any connection charging system has an important impact on the investment needed for that connection (basically expansion investment). Connection charging can involve:

- up-front payments by the user which clearly reduce the risk and cost of the investment to the operator; and/or
- on-going payments which reflect the costs of the investment, leaving some of the risks with the operator.

Deep versus Shallow Pricing

When choosing a pricing system there will be a decision as to how much of the costs associated with a specific user will actually be reflected in the charges that the user pays and how

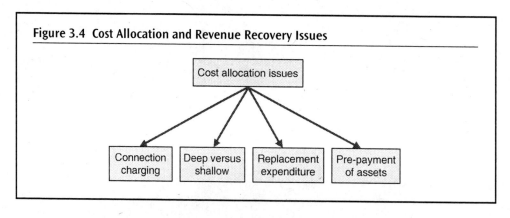

Figure 3.4 Cost Allocation and Revenue Recovery Issues

much is averaged across all users. This is often referred to as deep and shallow pricing—in deep pricing there is an attempt to determine as much of the direct and indirect costs caused by an individual user while shallow pricing limits itself to allocating only the most obvious direct costs associated with a user to that user. Clearly from an economic perspective it is better to charge users the costs that they actually cause but from a company risk perspective it is better to maximize the shared costs being allocated across all users so that the risk of losses arising from an individual user exiting the system are minimized (unless those costs are met through an up-front payment, exit guarantee or bond or some other mechanism and so do not create a risk for the operator).

Replacement Expenditure

In some situations, regulators have allowed capital expenditure to be recovered as operating expenditure. Case Study 9 in the Appendix outlines one example of this, taken from the gas sector in Great Britain, where a large program of replacement of the distribution network was being undertaken for health and safety reasons.[20] The approach taken by the regulator included allocating 50 percent of the replacement investment costs to operating expenditure rather than capital expenditure. This allocation was taken for two reasons: firstly it was felt that this reflected the allocation of benefits between existing and future consumers; and secondly ensuring sustainable price levels.

Pre-payment

Some major investments can take several years to be completed and operational. There is an issue as to whether existing users should meet some, or all, the costs associated with this ongoing investment—this is normally just a question as to whether assets in the course of construction should be included in the RAB although in extreme cases it could involve additional revenues being recovered prior to any construction starting. If these assets are included in the RAB before they become operational then existing users will be pre-paying some of the costs for future consumers.

Pre-payment is often linked to practical financing considerations for a company—if access to finance is limited, or the cost of funding becomes prohibitive, then "borrowing" from existing consumers may be an option.

Case Studies of the Regulatory Treatment of Investment

The Appendix presents a set of country case studies which detail how regulators have approached investment issues in the determination of price controls. These approaches show how in practice some of the main techniques described above have been implemented. The focus of the case study, for example on the particular approach towards regulating investment, is noted in the table.

---

20. This case study is also a good example of how unit costs can be pre-set and volumes left flexible when there is uncertainty about exactly what pipes are going to be replaced at what time. Unit costs were established for different pipe sizes.

CHAPTER 4

Assessment of Investment Approaches

I t is clear from the discussion in Chapters 2 and 3 that a single approach to investment may not provide adequate incentives in all the situations that a utility is likely to face. Yet, many regulators have chosen to focus on a single approach or, worse still, have not even articulated or expressed their approach to investment. The case study of Abu Dhabi provides an example where a regulator has adopted one dominant approach. It is also relatively common to find regulators having developed an approach to predicted investment, but without a clear approach to dealing with unpredictable investment.[21] So what approaches should a regulator use? This Chapter of the paper assesses the various approaches against a set of basic criteria. Chapter 5 provides suggestions on when different approaches could be used, depending upon the circumstances faced.

In order to assess the various approaches the following basic aspects will be considered:

- the risk allocation created by the approach;
- the impact on profitability, cash flows and other incentives for minimizing the cost of investments, including opportunities for gaming;
- the direct and indirect regulatory costs of the approach; and
- the ability to handle different types of investment.

The assessments provided here are of course generalizations, but they do provide a framework in which to understand the qualities of the different approaches. Each regulatory

---

21. For example, the National Electric Power Regulatory Authority of Pakistan (NEPRA) has now developed an approach to predictable investment in its price determinations, but is yet to develop an approach to unpredictable investment, although the latest determination does start to address this issue—NEPRA 2004.

regime is different and any assessment in practice will need to consider the minutiae of the regime. We consider first the different approaches as far as inclusion of assets in the regulatory asset base, and we then look at cost allocation and revenue issues.

Approaches to Inclusion of Assets in the Regulatory Asset Base

Risk Allocation

Table 4.1 provides a broad and illustrative overview of how the different approaches allocate cost and demand risks between operators and consumers.[22]

This table focuses on two elements for each of two key risks. For most of the approaches the risks associated with inclusion of the costs are handled up-front (meaning that the consumer bears this risk). Only for the ex-post based systems is the risk of inclusion faced by the operator, since investment is undertaken prior to regulatory approval and consequently there is a risk that some (or all) the cost of the investment will be rejected by the regulator and consequently become a cost for the operator and its shareholders, often referred to as stranded costs.[23] However, these ex-post systems do bring some risk mitigation for the operators: since there is no well established benchmark for the cost of the investment any cost overrun is harder to define. Consequently, consumers bear more of the cost overrun risk under ex-post based systems rather than the forward

Table 4.1 Risk Allocation of the Different Approaches

Approach	Cost risks Inclusion	Demand risks within the price control period Overruns	Below 100%
Ex-ante ex-post	Consumer	Operator	Mixed
Interim determination	Consumer	Operator	Mixed
Ex-post			
Logging-up	Operator	Consumer[1]	Mixed
Prudency Test	Operator	Mixed	Mixed
Contracting out	Consumer	Contractor	Mixed
Triggers	Consumer	Operator	Mixed

Notes: 1. Since there is no forecast figure against which the out-turn cost can be measured the consumer is bound to face the risks of inefficiency and cost overruns. This would change if a prudency test were included in the logging-up system.

22. The table does not consider broader obsolescence risk which is driven by the details of the broader regime.

23. There are several well documented examples of investment costs being 'stranded' this way in the US power sector. Most notably the wave of nuclear generation disallowals in the early 1980s and the chapter 11 proceedings for companies like the El Paso Electric Company and the Public Service Company of New Hampshire. These and other such examples are well documented in Sidak and Spulber (1998).

looking ex-ante ex-post or interim determination where any cost overrun is the responsibility of the operator.[24]

When looking at demand risks the story is less clear. The overall form of price control has an important impact on allocating demand risk. For example, a revenue-cap would ensure that consumers face all the demand risks while a price-cap would shift risk associated with deviations from forecast demand onto the operator. Therefore, in almost all the systems considered, the risk that demand during the price control period is less than 100 percent is only partly addressed through the regulation of investment. This is partly because the impacts of less than 100 percent utilization depend on several factors. It may be known that initially demand is less than capacity but this is due to the lumpiness of investments (the Terminal 5 investment at Heathrow airport, set out in case study 15 is a prime example of this), but it is still possible that actual demand will deviate from forecast demand. Under an ex-ante ex-post system the consumer faces the risks associated with planned insufficient demand, as the agreed cost of the investment is included in the RAB and returns are earned by the operator. However, the overall impact on the operator will depend on the broader price control structure, as noted earlier.

Whether obsolescence risk is faced by the operator depends primarily on whether the RAB is periodically reassessed for optimality. Regulatory regimes that have the RAB periodically reassessed for optimality introduce substantial risks related to obsolescence, as determined by the regulator. In the electricity transmission system in Australia (case study 4) the use of an asset valuation system that every five years assesses the optimality of investments has created risks of assets being written-down. Another example of the risks imposed by such reviews comes from the power sector in Brazil, where a recent decision by the regulator on the level of the RAB has included a provision to write off investments that are not expected to be utilized in the next ten years, with no apparent corresponding allowance for the loss of investor value.[25] While it could be argued that it is unreasonable to expect consumers to bear the costs of these investments, the possibility or use of such approaches clearly place more risks on operators.

Contracting out approaches can reduce the risks of inclusion of an investment for an operator, provided that a competitive process is followed and the cost of the asset will be accepted. Much of the cost overrun risks are also likely to be passed on to the contractor, although some may be retained by the utility. The allocation of demand risks will be similar to the approaches discussed earlier. These approaches, such as the Peruvian electricity transmission system (case study 12) and the Scottish water projects (case study 13) ensure that the assets are included in the RAB. Another example, not covered in the case studies, can be found in India where there is a move to involve the private sector in electricity transmission through BOT type projects. These have the advantage of establishing a tariff for the life of the asset rather than just the next price control period, the latter

---

24. There are examples where exogenous elements of investment costs are allowed on a cost pass-through basis, for example, exchange rate related cost elements. There are some examples where overruns have been allowed once a prudency test has been applied.

25. Discussed in more detail in Chapter 3. Also, see Foster and Antmann (2004) for a more detailed discussion of this issue in Brazil.

being the approach adopted by the regulator when POWERGRID, the state-owned transmission company, undertakes investments.[26]

In summary, ex-post approaches place greater risk on the operator since they have less certainty about whether the investment costs will be allowed. This has been identified in other papers as one of the major concerns with traditional rate of return regulation and something that has hampered private participation in developing and transitional economies—it is also one of the arguments in favor of performance-based regulation (for example, Alexander 2003).

Impact on Profitability, Cash Flows and Other Incentives

A key aspect of the regulatory regime for investment has to be the incentives that it creates for companies to both actually undertake the investment and to do it an efficient manner (capital expenditure savings). This incentive can be considered in two ways:

- the potential impact on the profitability of the activity; and
- the variability introduced into the cash flows.

While the profitability element should, in principle, be the only element that matters, the reality for companies operating in any country, developed or developing, is that cash flow can be more important. Guaranteed, unvarying cash flow with a lower level of profitability will often be more acceptable than a higher level of profitability but variable cash flow, especially when access to the financial markets is limited or expensive. Consequently, any investment regime has to be considered in terms of both aspects.

The first aspect of this assessment is between the two 'extreme' approaches, ex-ante ex-post approach and ex-post systems (the interim determination approach will deliver a result that lies between these two). Consider Figure 4.2, this shows the cash flow impact of the two approaches. For the ex-ante ex-post approach the returns (profits and depreciation) on the investment start to accrue from the time that the investment is expected to become operational. With logging-up, the operator must bear the financing charges until the investment can be incorporated into the RAB at the next price determination—in this case four years later. Consequently, even if these carrying costs are incorporated, as in Abu Dhabi (but incorporation is not necessarily the case in logging-up—see OFWAT's logging-up system in case study 7) and the profitability of the company protected, there is a marked difference in the profile of the Net Present Value (NPV)—shown in Table 4.2 and Figure 4.1.

Consequently, while over the lifetime of the asset the two approaches may be revenue neutral, there is a clear cash flow difference which could have a significant impact on the company. This is shown in Figure 4.1 where the costs associated with the investment are initially borne by the company in all cases except the ex-ante ex-post and consequently

---

26. The general approach followed in India is described in case study 10. Specific issues relating to the Build-Own-Operate approach to private involvement are described in a forthcoming paper by the South Asia Energy and Infrastructure Unit of the World Bank. Interestingly, joint ventures between the private sector and POWERGRID are treated like POWERGRID investments rather than BOTs by the regulator.

Table 4.2 Illustrative NPV Impact of Logging-up

NPV over	Ex-ante/ex-post	Logging-up	Logging-up (no carrying-costs allowed)
5 years	47.5	(47.5)	(47.5)
10 years	86.4	14.6	(8.7)

Note: ( ) Denotes a negative value. Based on an asset with an assumed 20 year life.

even when the initial costs are recovered in later years, the company has to meet the cash flow implications for the first control period.

So, from this it would appear that where investments can be forecast a stronger incentive to invest is created by the ex-ante ex-post approach than the other approaches. The incentives are stronger if companies are allowed to keep the gains for a longer period—as noted in Chapter 3 there are several variants of the ex-ante ex-post approach—as illustrated in Figure 4.2. The figure illustrates the impact of the variants by measuring the NPV of each relative to a base variant—the fixed five year approach (option 1).

Figure 4.2 shows, not unexpectedly, that the greatest incentive for minimizing the actual cost of investment relative to the forecast level is created when the inclusion of the actual investment figures in place of the forecast ones happens at the second next

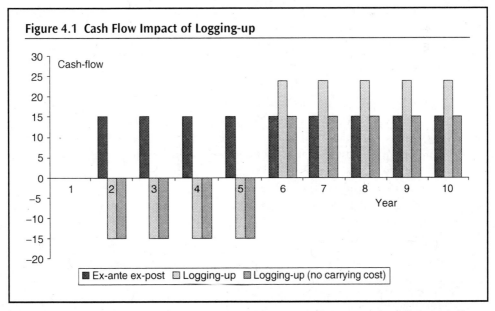

Figure 4.1 Cash Flow Impact of Logging-up

Note: Simplifying assumptions are made for this figure, and it should be treated as being purely illustrative. An investment of 100 is assumed to occur in period 1 and the operator faces a regulatory price control period of five years. The allowed rate of return is assumed to be 10% and the life of the asset is 20 years.

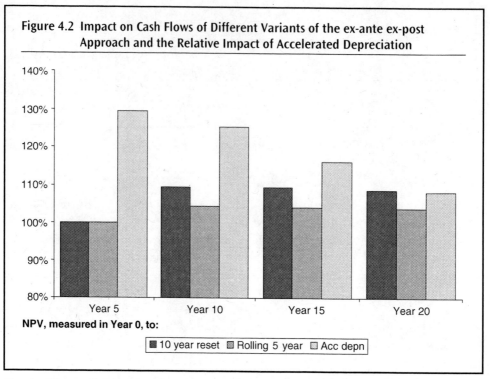

Figure 4.2 Impact on Cash Flows of Different Variants of the ex-ante ex-post Approach and the Relative Impact of Accelerated Depreciation

Note: in this example it is assumed that the company needs to invest 100 each year—so the impact here is a cumulative one. This magnifies the impact when compared to the simple example provided in Figure 4.1 but is also a closer reflection of the reality of multi-period investments with some being reset sooner after investment occurs than others.

price determination—the fixed 10 year approach (option 2).[27] The rolling five-year approach (option 3) lies between the other two options.

To provide a benchmark for the significance of the results a final NPV figure is also calculated—using the base option 1 ex-ante ex-post approach but then incorporating accelerated depreciation (in the example the standard asset life is 20 years and the accelerated life is 10 years).[28] As can be seen from the figure, utilizing accelerated depreciation has the potential to yield a more significant cash flow impact, although this will of course depend on the degree of acceleration that is allowed.

The incentives for capital efficiency can be considerable. OFWAT have estimated that efficiency savings of up to 30 percent in quality enhancement programmes, and savings of up to 15 percent in capital maintenance expenditure have been achieved in the water sector in the UK.[29] In July 2004 the ACCC issued a speech setting out arguments for moving

27. The degree of divergence between the options obviously depends on the assumptions made and actual outcomes will change this. However, if no unanticipated capex efficiency savings were made all that would happen is that the three options would all yield the same result.

28. An analysis of the impact of changing the rate of accelerated depreciation is presented later in this Chapter.

29. Figure 17, page 25 of NAO (2002).

away from the ex-post system currently employed towards a primarily ex-ante system.[30] One of the arguments put forward was that "… it improves incentive for transmission companies to invest in the most efficient projects."

Although they create incentives for savings in capital, ex-ante systems also raise the problem of companies proposing investments and then not undertaking them. Where possible, it is important to link the investments to observable outputs. When there is a question as to whether a company will undertake investments one partial solution is to use the positive trigger system, as described in Chapter 3, which links the increase in revenues to compensate for the costs of investment with the actual delivery of the investment. This system is used in the Argentine gas sector.

Finally, we assess the opportunities for gaming under each of the approaches. Gaming, as described in Chapter 3, reflects companies reacting to perverse incentives in the

---

Table 4.3 The Allocation of Risks and the Creation of Incentives—Lessons from the Case Studies

Approach	Lessons
Ex-ante ex-post	In the vast majority of cases a simple fixed five year restatement process is used. Only in the England and Wales water and sewerage case has another option been considered and then employed which is a rolling five-year approach.
Interim determinations	Several of the case studies have interim determinations, most with materiality thresholds, such as those in Chile. When unexpected but significant expenditures can occur, such as with environmentally driven investments in the water industry, significant utilization of the approach can be seen—this is the case in England and Wales.
Ex-post	Each of the logging-up systems incorporates some form of prudency test and that has been employed by regulators. In terms of the actual experience with respect to amount of investment delivered:
	▪ In Abu Dhabi it can be seen that the amount of capex delivered under the logging-up system for one company was greater than the capex forecast for the price control period. However, this may be as much a reflection of the poor forecasting in 1999 as the incentive impact of the approach since the evidence from the other two companies was of actual capex spend significantly lower than forecast.
	▪ In the case of the water and sewerage industry in England and Wales no allowance for carrying-costs is made and consequently companies are incentivised to minimize investment that is subject to logging-up (or to maximize it so that an interim determination is brought about). It should also be noted that the vast majority of investment in this sector falls under the ex-ante ex-post approach—for example, less than 10% was captured through logging-up between 1994 and 1999.
	The water and sewerage companies in Manila face a similar situation.

---

30. Willett (2004). See also case study 4.

regulatory system. Often the perverse incentives arise from the detail of the system rather than the broad category—this reflects the fact that the 'devil is in the detail' and choosing a generic approach is insufficient, the detail of the regime is what drives the incentives, perverse or otherwise. Of course, companies may not actually undertake this gaming, but the possibility exists.

Ex-ante ex-post systems face two types of gaming:

- overestimating the investment needed to provide additional revenues during the price control period; and
- postponing planned investments, especially towards the end of a price control period, to maximise the positive incentives.

Given these concerns regulators are often compelled to include:

- benchmarking of investment costs to ensure padding of costs is limited;
- output or outcome measures linked to the investments so overestimates are harder to justify; and
- ex-post assessments of actual investments to establish whether necessary investments were undertaken etc.

An example of the last approach is provided in the review by the Office of Regulation for Electricity and Gas (OFREG) and the Monopolies and Mergers Commission of the capital expenditure program for the first price control period applied to Northern Ireland Electricity (NIE). They found that some of the investment "efficiency" was actually related to management being focused elsewhere (privatization) and so not undertaking the investment. This led to a £25m clawback—amounting to one third of the investment "efficiency" for years two to four of the price control period.[31]

Interim determinations also create incentives for gaming, although these are mostly determined by the actual approach. Possibly the most important gaming aspect of the interim determination is the question of how a regulator will react—in Manila the first interim determination involved significant risk for the operator with respect to uncertainty as to how the regulator would actually undertake the determination.

With the ex-post systems there are other types of gaming possible. Depending on the perceived risks of a logging-up system, especially if it is part of a broader regime incorporating other approaches depending on the materiality of the investment, there can be incentives to maximize investment so that the uncertainty of the logging-up system is replaced with another approach—such as an interim determination. Of course, the incentives to game will actually depend on the alternative approach to investment that is available. In the water industry in England and Wales there is greater certainty attached to utilization of the interim determination approach than logging-up, so companies may try to push past the materiality threshold. Further, since the carrying costs associated with logging-up are not remunerated in the OFWAT system this creates an even greater incentive to maximize investment if it will breach the materiality threshold. Otherwise the investment will be minimized as a way of limiting the exposure to carrying costs.

---

31. See especially pages 28–30 and chapter 7 of the Monopolies and Mergers Commission (1997).

Regulatory Costs

What compliance costs are created under each of the approaches? Two sets of costs need to be considered:

- the direct costs to the regulator of operating the system; and
- the costs for the operator of preparing submissions etc.

Table 4.4 sets out some observations on the likely costs associated with each of the main approaches. While direct evidence on the costs for companies and regulators of the different approaches is not easily available, it is possible to derive some implications from a consideration of the usage of the approaches. If these observations are summarized into

Table 4.4 Compliance Costs

Approach	Direct costs for the regulator	Operator compliance costs
Ex-ante ex-post	Need to undertake reviews of planned investments as part of the price determination. No within price control costs unless a rolling adjustment system is followed when there would be an annual need to revisit the RAB.	Need to provide investment forecasts at the price review and then keep a tally of the actual investment costs so that the ex-post resetting can occur.
Interim determinations	Need to undertake a review of the investment issues as and when an interim determination is called. Since this would not be at the time of the main price determination it is likely that the costs would be higher than undertaking the review as part of the main price determination. However, the type of investment being assessed is likely to have an impact on the associated workload and consequently the direct costs could be quite variable.	As with the regulator, the operator faces the problem of handling this outside the main price determination process. There is also the need to demonstrate the materiality of the costs so that the interim determination can be initiated (checking this is an additional cost for the regulator).
Ex-post	The cost for the regulator will depend in part on the type of ex-post system employed. - With logging-up there will be only a limited cost since the evaluation will take place at the next price determination. - A prudency review will require more resources since the assessments made by the company will have to be evaluated and since it is after the fact there will always be time spent in finding answers, understanding why things were done in a certain way, etc.	For the company there will be additional costs in terms of: - keeping detailed logs of the additional investments undertaken; and - keeping documentation necessary for the prudency review.

Table 4.5 Summary on Compliance Costs

Approach	Direct costs for the regulator	Operator compliance costs
Ex-ante ex-post	Low	Low
Interim determinations	Medium/High	Medium
Ex-post	Medium/High	Medium

an overall assessment of the costs (whether they are high, medium or low), an evaluation like that set out in Table 4.5 could be found.

The prevalence of interim determinations as a type of approach and the usage that has been made, especially in the water and sewerage industry in England and Wales suggests that although this may be a relatively expensive system, it is an approach that is cost effective. The 12 applications made in England and Wales only saw two rejected on materiality grounds—this suggests that the companies, if given adequate guidelines, are more than capable of determining the materiality element and so limiting the cost for the regulator.

In the Manila water and sewerage industry the first interim determination took over two years to complete since this was the first test of the regulatory system enshrined in the contract. While this was a significant cost, it should be a one-off and allow the future periodic reviews to be less time consuming because many of the key issues that would have to be debated have been discussed.

There is also some external evidence supportive of this assessment. This includes the recent ACCC speech (see footnote 39) which included the following statement:

> … It's also a very complicated task for the ACCC to determine, as it requires detailed analysis of the need for the project, technical specification and costs and benefits of each project at the time that the investment is made.

A study of cost drivers for energy regulation in developing countries found some evidence supporting the fact that regulatory institutions with performance-based regulation tend to have fewer staff (Domah, Pollitt, and Stern 2002). Because performance regulation on the whole is linked with ex-ante ex-post type approaches to investment, this evidence is supportive of the proposal that direct regulatory costs are lower for those approaches to regulating investment.

Ability to Handle Different Types of Investment

The final criteria to consider is the ability of each of the approaches to handle the different forms of investment identified in Chapter 2 of the paper.

Table 4.6 provides an overview of the way in which each approach handles the two basic forms of investment—those that are predictable (primarily maintenance and rehabilitation investment but also some expansion and quality investment) and those that are not predictable (primarily quality and expansion investment).

There is some evidence from the case studies that can help illustrate these points. What is clear from the ex-ante ex-post examples is that the systems are unable to handle investments that cannot be predicted—this was also high-lighted in the Pakistan case study at the beginning of this chapter. Interim determinations, as used in Chile, Manila and the water and sewerage sector in England and Wales are clearly aimed at dealing with costs that

Table 4.6 Ability to Handle Different Types of Investment

Approach	Predictable	Not predictable
Ex-ante ex-post	Well placed to address this type of investment given the forecastability of this type.	Where it is possible to forecast the quality and expansion investments then this approach is well suited. Where these types of investment cannot be forecast at the time of the price determination then this approach is poor at handling the investment.
Interim determinations	This approach is not well suited for this type of investment and is not needed.	Where these types of investment cannot be forecast and are significant when they occur, this approach is well suited. For example, major environmental legal changes leading to big investments could be well handled by this approach.
Ex-post	Ex-post approaches are not well placed to handle this approach owing to the amount of investment that would have to be handled.	Logging-up type approaches can be well placed to handle these types of investments. For significant investments these approaches may not be so well suited owing to the risks and cash flow implications discussed earlier in the chapter.

cannot be predicted at a standard price determination—say movements in exchange rates, construction costs, environmental investments, and so forth. A good example of the way in which logging-up can be used to handle all types of investment is shown by the Abu Dhabi case study (summarised in Box 4.1). In other case studies logging-up has a much more focused usage, small scale difficult to predict investments.

Two further case studies are worth high-lighting for the way in which they seek to overcome some of the uncertainty linked with investment.

First, the Error-Correction Mechanism (ECM) utilized by the National Grid Company in England and Wales (case study 8) was designed to handle a situation where the unit cost of the investment was "known" (or predictable) but the volume was uncertain. In this case the volume was an exogenous factor determined by the number of new generator connections requested over the life of the price control. The regulator forecast that an "average" connection would cost £20m per GW and introduced a system whereby each GW of generation connection over the base of allowed connections would be remunerated at this average cost. Consequently the need for regulatory involvement was simplified while allowing the flexibility to handle uncertain investment volume. This system subsequently faced some problems inasmuch as the "average" was felt to be inappropriate given the increasing number of smaller renewable generation connections being requested.

Second, within the gas system in Great Britain a major rehabilitation and replacement program of investment was recently mandated on health and safety grounds (case study 9). The exact type of pipe being replaced could not be forecast with total certainty and so a system whereby unit costs for different sizes of pipe were agreed and then any deviations

---

Box 4.1 Dealing with Data Problems—Lessons from Abu Dhabi

Regulation is still in the process of being developed in the water and electricity sectors in Abu Dhabi. One area that has attracted significant attention is that of investment. While it was clear that investment was needed, the planning systems for the state-owned companies were not in a position to deliver credible forecasts for the life of the price-control that was being prepared.

Consequently, rather than create spurious incentives and possible future problems the regulator decided to impose a logging-up system on all investment for the first three-year price control period with a prudency test to be applied at the next price control review to assess and allow the efficiently incurred capital expenditure. This helped create certainty for the companies as to how the investment would be treated but allowed the flexibility needed to handle the uncertainty about investment needs.

How well did this work? In the case of one company greater investment than had been expected at the price determination was undertaken, even with the regulator's established prudency test. This may be a reflection of poor capex forecasting or an indication of the company's perception of the regulator's future capital expenditure efficiency assessment. In fact, for the other two companies the actual capex provisionally allowed by the regulator at the next price control review were significantly lower than expected. This tends to confirm the capex forecasting problem rather than any incentive to over or inefficiently spend per se. Carrying costs created by the logging-up approach were allowed and the fact that the companies are state-owned may have helped address any cash flow concerns.

Could this approach be adopted elsewhere—especially with private companies? The answer is clearly a tradeoff between the accuracy of the information available at the price determination, the cash flow implications of using logging-up, the length of the price control period and the credibility of the regulator/regulatory rules. What is clear is that this is a pragmatic answer to the ever present problem of a lack of information—it may be hard to make it the only way of handling investment but it is clearly far superior to having no system whatsoever!

Subsequently at the latest price review the regulator adopted an approach that is moving towards the ex-ante ex-post approach since provisional allowances for investment, based on company forecasts, have been incorporated into the revenue calculations.

Source: Case study 1.

from the base line replacement program could be assessed against this set of agreed costs. Again, flexibility was being allowed for the company to react as needed while controls were being put in place to limit the need for detailed ex-post assessments.

Assessment of Cost Allocation and Revenue Recovery Issues

As noted in Chapter 3, there are three cost allocation and revenue issues that also deserve attention:

- connection charging—specifically, degree of consumer contribution, and deep versus shallow attribution of costs—and
- general pre-payment/revenue advancement.[32]

---

32. Customer contributions are a form of prepayment but the aspect being captured here is general pre-payment by all consumers through the pricing system rather than pre-payment for a customer specific asset by the customer.

A small number of the case studies focus on these issues—especially Argentine water (case study 2), England and Wales electricity transmission (case study 8), India electricity transmission (case study 10), UK airports (case study 15), and gas distribution in Great Britain (case study 9). These issues are evaluated against the same basic set of criteria set out above, although the regulatory cost criteria has not been considered since it has much less significance for these issues.

Risk Allocation

When thinking about the risk allocation impact of the three pricing issues it is useful to focus on the same two basic aspects of risk, costs, and demand.

Customer contributions can have a major impact on cost risks. If the customer is expected to meet a significant proportion of the connection charge then it is the specific customer that is effectively taking the risk associated with the asset—the only real question is whether the asset is being included in the depreciation base.[33] Who faces the risk of an overrun depends on the type of agreement embodied in the connection charge—if it is a fixed price contract then the operator faces the risk while if it is a time and materials contract then the consumer faces the risks. Of course, if a low level of customer contribution is required then the risk allocation follows that set out in Table 4.1.

With high customer contributions the demand risk is held by the specific consumer since they have already covered the costs of the connection assets. Again, if low customer contributions are being made the risk will depend on the more general regulatory rules for investment evaluated in Table 4.1.

The 'depth' of the charging for the connection assets is also important. Deep charging is when as many of the assets associated with connecting a consumer to a network are allocated to the specific consumer, shallow is when only the most direct assets associated with the connection are allocated. Under both approaches the more general regulatory approach to investment will drive the allocation of risk for costs. However, combining deep connection charging with a high customer contribution clearly shifts more risk on to the specific customer than shallow charging with high customer contributions.

Deep charging does shift some of the demand risks onto the specific customer, no matter what degree of customer contribution is required (although, again, the mixture of deep charging and high customer contributions clearly magnifies the demand risks being borne by the customer). What does need to be considered when thinking about deep charging is the ability to link specific assets with specific users. While the principle of deep charging may sound appealing the practicality of applying it may pose significant problems—the case study on transmission charging in England and Wales (case study 8) is an example where the regulator is moving away from deep charging—discussed further below.

As with the deep or shallow charging system, general pre-payment or revenue advancement for future assets through the pricing system has an affect on the demand risks.

---

33. Of course, the broader regulatory rules concerning connection charging, such as the degree of contestability, whether regulated prices exist etc have a key impact. However, for large users and major input providers, such as generators to a transmission system, the rules are likely to be more flexible with the price being a negotiated affair.

If existing consumers are paying for assets that will be utilized by future consumers—such as an airport terminal (the case in the UK for Heathrow's Terminal 5, explained in case study 15) then they are effectively shifting some of the potential underutilization risk from either future consumers or the operator. Equally, if an asset proves to be obsolete that has been fully or partly prepaid, say through accelerated depreciation such as used in India (case study 10) then part of that obsolescence risk is being borne by the existing consumers that are making the pre-payment.

Table 4.7 summarizes the risk allocation for the cost allocation and revenue issues.

What are the lessons from the case studies? With respect to connection charging in England and Wales the existing deep connection charging system is perceived to lack transparency and leave consumers at the risk of decisions by other consumers where they share assets and consequently a move to shallower charging is being proposed. The Argentine electricity transmission regulatory system (case study 3) for investment is another example of connection charging—the customers who would benefit from the new transmission lines are responsible for payment.

Pre-payment or revenue advancement has only been utilized in a few of the case studies. However, what is clear is that some of the uses have been driven by risk issues. In the Indian electricity sector accelerated depreciation was utilized as a way of ensuring that companies had sufficient cash flow to meet financing costs and repay debt—so lowering their risks (this was further reinforced in the 2004 CERC determination when the asset life for accelerated depreciation was reduced from 12 to 10 years). Second, passing the funding of T5 at Heathrow airport to consumers was perceived as a way of reducing the already incrementally high risks (see Box 3.1 for a discussion of the higher returns allowed for T5) for the operator.

Finally, the use of pay-as-you-go (another name effectively for customer contributions, but in this case shared across all existing consumers) approach adopted for the replacement of iron gas mains in Great Britain is another example of pre-payment. Part of the conscious decision by the regulator to pass 50 percent of the investment costs to the existing consumers as a direct contribution was that existing consumers would benefit from the improved health and safety arising from the replaced pipes but would not pay a

Table 4.7 Risk Allocation of the Different Cost Allocation and Revenue Approaches

Approach	Cost risks		Demand risks during the price control period	
	Inclusion	Overruns	Below 100%	Obsolescence
Degree of customer contribution to connection charging (high/low)	Specific customer/ Mixed[1]	Operator and/or consumer/ Mixed[1]	Specific customer/ Mixed[1]	Specific consumer/ Mixed[1]
Connection charging (deep/ shallow)	Mixed[1]	Mixed[1]	Specific customer/ Mixed[1]	Mixed[1] customer/ Mixed[1]
General pre-payment/ revenue advancement	Mixed[1]	Mixed[1]	Existing customers	Existing customers

Notes: 1. This depends on the approach to regulating investment being adopted as per table 4.1.

corresponding amount if the whole investment cost was treated in the normal way of being included in the RAB.

One general concern with both pre-payment and significant connection charging systems does need to be addressed. For residential consumers significant up-front payments may be unaffordable—or require a borrowing cost that is significantly above that of the company. As such, thought does need to be given to whether any proposals are "fair" or affordable. It may be the case that industrial and commercial consumers can face more significant up-front charges than residential consumers and tariffs should be designed accordingly. When designing a system this is something that the regulator, Government and operator should determine.

Impact on Profitability, Cash Flows and Other Incentives

Customer contributions (whether for connections or some form of general pre-payment) clearly improve the cash flows of the operator and leave the profitability unchanged. In this sense they are no different to accelerated depreciation, except that the acceleration is total. As seen earlier in this Chapter, accelerated depreciation can have a major impact on the cash flows of a business—especially when compared to some of the other approaches available for regulating investment.

The actual impact of accelerated depreciation depends on the degree of acceleration. Figure 4.3 illustrates this by showing the NPV of cash flows at different time periods for different degrees of acceleration—in each case measured as a percentage of the base case (depreciation over the normal life of the asset). Unsurprisingly, what is clear is that the shorter the period for depreciation the greater the impact on cash flow. Also, the cash flow profile is strongly affected by the choice of depreciation, shown by the measures of the impact over different time periods.

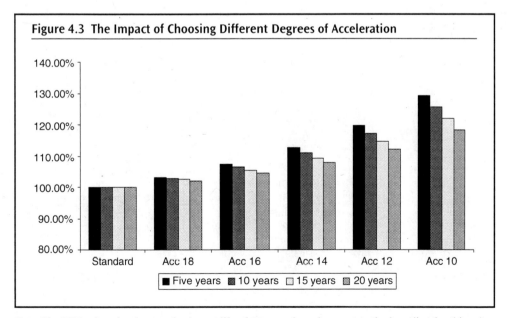

Figure 4.3 The Impact of Choosing Different Degrees of Acceleration

Note: The NPV values for the standard asset life of 20 years have been set as the base-line for this calculation and allocated values of 100%. All other NPVs are illustrated as relative to this base-line.

What does this do to incentives? Pre-payment if anything makes incentives more straight-forward since it mitigates the pressure for shifting what should be investment expenditures into operating expenditure (a general gaming issue discussed in Chapter 3).

Whether customer contributions like the gas distribution pay-as-you-go approach create incentives for greater investment is not clear. On the one hand they allocate a significant proportion of the costs directly to consumers and so limit the funding needs and risks faced by the company—the concern that a future regulator will allow a rate of return below the cost of funds actually incurred by the company will still exist, but it applies to a smaller investment base. When accessing external funds is difficult for a company then this type of pay-as-you-go system can help overcome that problem.

Accelerated depreciation can have the same type of impact on incentives as customer contributions—especially when the problem faced is one of access to long-term finance. Being forced to borrow money at a maturity less than that assumed by the regulator creates a refinancing risk for the operator which may lead it to minimize investments. By at least allowing repayment of the shorter-maturity loans through this accelerated depreciation the operator should be expected to undertake the required level of investment.

Ability to Handle Different Types of Investment

Customer contributions for connection charging should be equally applicable to predictable or unpredictable investments. However, connection charging only really makes sense in terms of service expansion—not maintenance/rehabilitation or quality improvements.

Table 4.8 Ability to Handle Different Types of Investment

Approach	Predictable	Not predictable
Customer contributions	When applied to connection charging this approach only makes sense for service expansion.	When applied to connection charging this approach only makes sense for service expansion.
	Quality and maintenance/rehabilitation investments can benefit from customer contributions although asking specific consumers to make contributions would seem to make sense for predictable investments (except for large consumers).	Quality and maintenance/rehabilitation investments can benefit from customer contributions although asking specific consumers to make contributions would seem to make sense for predictable investments (except for large consumers).
Deep or shallow	Deep charging is able to handle any type of investment, although it is better suited to predictable investments.	Deep charging is able to handle unpredictable investments but it could create great volatility in prices.
General pre-payment	Since these systems tend to require inclusion into the general pricing system they are better suited to handle predictable investments—although as shown by the gas distribution example other elements of a regulatory investment system can be introduced to address unpredictable investments.	

This is also true of the deep versus shallow argument—although there is some more relevance to maintenance/rehabilitation issues and quality improvements. More general customer contributions can apply to other forms of investment although this is less frequently used (pay-as-you-go can be considered as a form of general customer contribution rather than a specific customer contribution).

Pre-payment/revenue advancement approaches are, however, more generally applicable to predictable investments. For example, the pay-as-you-go approach adopted for gas distribution in Great Britain is being utilized for a quality improvement. Service expansion for airport services in the UK are being pre-paid by existing consumers—something also being utilized for the new international airport in Bangkok, Thailand (Pricewaterhouse-Coopers 2003). Finally, the accelerated depreciation in the Indian electricity transmission system is being used to fund all types of investment. Unpredictable investments are harder to handle through these pre-payment systems since the investment needs to be incorporated into the price control for the period. Table 4.8 summarizes this assessment of the approaches to handling different types of investment.

CHAPTER 5

Designing a Regulatory System to Handle Investment

One of the clear lessons from Chapter 4 is that some systems are better at handling certain situations and circumstances. Consequently, it is now possible to consider what lessons can be drawn for the design of regulatory systems.

As shown in Chapters 2 and 4 different types of investment have different characteristics which require different regulatory approaches. Figure 5.1 captures this by showing what options appear best suited under different situations.

Why has this set of options been suggested? In each case one or more approach to incorporating investment into the regulatory system has been proposed based on the situation being faced. For example, when investment is unpredictable and the company either has cash flow considerations or faces investments with a material impact on the finances of the company, then the system best suited for that type of investment is likely to be based on interim determinations. Large predictable investments are, however, better suited to either a contracting-out approach or an ex-ante ex-post regime (possibly with positive or negative triggers linked to the delivery of the investment).

From this it can be seen that a portfolio of approaches might well work best when multiple types of investment are faced—although it is, of course, important to ensure that whatever portfolio is chosen is kept as simple as possible to limit compliance costs and minimize distortions to incentives for investment. This is reinforced by the evidence from some of the regulators that have put in place multiple systems owing to the range of investments that their sectors face—Box 5.1 summarizes this from the perspective of the water and sewerage industry in England and Wales (a similar situation is seen in the water and sewerage sector in Manila).

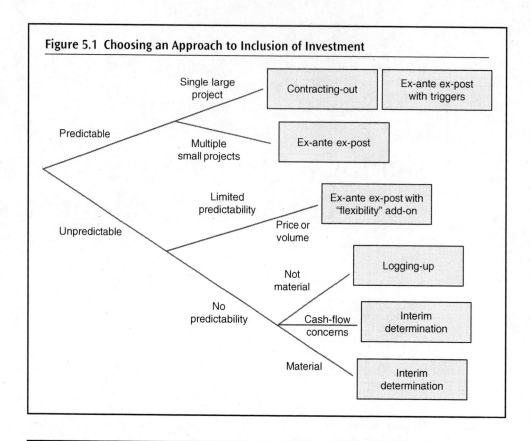

Figure 5.1 Choosing an Approach to Inclusion of Investment

Box 5.1 Water and Sewerage in England and Wales—A Holistic Approach to Investment

When the water and sewerage industry in England and Wales was privatized in 1989 it was known that investment was going to be a major issue—environmental standards were being tightened with significant implications for the private companies. These standards continued to be tightened over the first 15 years of private ownership and around £50 billion of investment has taken place—compared to an equity sale price of around £5 billion at privatization.

During the 15 years OFWAT, the regulator, has established a comprehensive system for dealing with investment—covering all possibilities and ensuring incentives exist where it is possible to do so. This system includes:

- a base system of ex-ante ex-post regulation for investment handling the vast majority of investment. This system involves detailed forecasting and efficiency assessments at the price determination stage;

- a logging-up system to handle small scale unforeseen investments (although no carrying-costs are allowed for inclusion in the required revenue); and

- an interim determination system to handle larger unforeseen investments—based on materiality and type of investment.

This holistic approach has created a situation in which the range of possible types of investment are captured with clear rules and processes. The fact that carrying-costs for logging-up are not allowed is a potential handicap, although the fact that the cost is capped through the existence of the interim determination system does limit this downside.

Source: Case study 7.

In some cases there are several options best suited to dealing with a type of investment—such as the situation with single large predictable investments. Then the decision as to which approach to adopt can depend on:

- further regulatory cost concerns—running a single contracting-out auction may not make sense, but when there are several to be undertaken it may be worthwhile; and
- pragmatic concerns such as the cash flow implications of one approach over another—for example, contracting-out places less of a cash flow burden on the incumbent operator.

Are there cases where a single approach to regulating investment will be appropriate? It is unlikely that only one approach will ever be able to handle the range of types of investment faced by a sector and the various characteristics of those investments (as described in Chapter 2). Consequently it is likely that two or more approaches will be needed to create a regime that is able to address this range of types of investment—Box 5.1 provides a good example of such a holistic approach. Of course, it is also important to ensure that the regime does not become too complex—that can lead to high compliance costs as well as enhanced opportunities for gaming. There are examples of single approach systems—Box 4.1 provides the example of Abu Dhabi which utilized a single approach for the first price control period. However, the unique circumstances facing the regulator in Abu Dhabi at that time also have to be taken into account—unreliable data and state-owned companies with access to finance. Would a private operator have been able to finance investment under this regime? Or would a state-owned company that faces financing and cash flow constraints been able to operate under such a regime? Clearly the specific situation facing the sector needs to be taken into account when designing the regime but it is unlikely that a single approach will suffice in all but the rarest circumstances.

The pragmatic concerns noted above lead to a second set of options that need to be considered, those relating to cost allocations and revenue. Figure 5.2 sets out various circumstances that may be faced by the operator and our assessment of the best-practice options.

As noted in Chapter 4, some of these proposals need to be evaluated carefully. While high up-front payments, either in the form of customer contributions or pre-payment, may appear to be a solution to the situation faced, there may be issues relating to equity and affordability which could have an impact on the choice of approach. As such, the options high-lighted in Figure 5.2 should be seen as a starting point—much more situation specific evaluation would be required before a final decision regarding an approach could be taken. Further, ensuring that the interaction with the broader regulatory regime and the tariff structure/pricing system is appropriate for any proposal is important.

Of course, having chosen the options that are to be followed is only the beginning of the process—as noted previously, "the devil is in the detail." There are elements that should be included in each of the approaches—these are outlined below. In all cases it is important to:

- be clear as to what investment the approach is being applied to;
- keep the system as simple as possible—complexity carries many costs and risks;

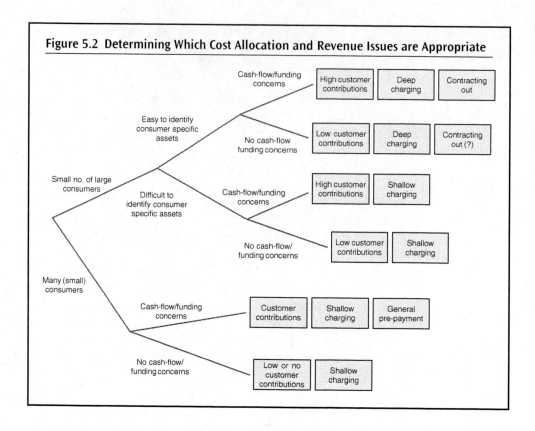

Figure 5.2 Determining Which Cost Allocation and Revenue Issues are Appropriate

- ensure that any games for operating expenditure/capital expenditure tradeoffs are addressed; and
- make, where possible, a very clear *ex ante* link between the investment and an outcome.[34]

What Should an Ex-ante Ex-post System Incorporate?

With an ex-ante ex-post system it is necessary to:

- Be clear about the period over which the operator can benefit from the efficiency savings—is it a fixed or rolling period, over how many years, and so forth. This will depend on the degree of incentive that is needed.
- Establish clearly the form of ex-post assessment that will take place (see below).

Additionally, it is important to provide where possible flexibility and allow tradeoffs to be made in the investment programs actually implemented by the companies, something that the proposed Australian only ex-ante approach provides.

---

34. If a company can deliver the outcome without needing to undertake the investment then that is all for the good–but at the planning stage there should be a link whenever possible between a desired outcome and the investments needed to deliver that outcome.

What Approach to Ex-post Assessment Should be Followed?

Box 3.3 sets out the proposals from IPART in New South Wales, Australia, as to what a prudency review should incorporate. This illustrates that it is important to have a set of rules by which prudency reviews will be undertaken, these should include:

- Focusing on information available at the time of taking the decision—hindsight is wonderful but creates significant risk.
- Consistency within the regime—if there is to be a risk of stranding will other actions be taken, such as a financial capital maintenance approach to depreciation that will mitigate the stranding risks.
- Consistency with industry "best practice" over issues such as safety standards, demand forecasting, and so forth.

What Elements Should be Incorporated into a 'Flexibility' Add-on?

In some circumstances it is possible that some aspects of the hard to predict forms of investment may be predictable—say either the unit price or the volume (but not both!) If that is the case, some issues to consider include:

- The degree of certainty about the unit price (or multiple unit prices as used in the gas replacement system in Great Britain)—if it is difficult to predict the unit cost with any certainty the approach will not provide conditions conducive to investment. Case study 8, electricity transmission in England and Wales, provides a good example of where the simple unit cost has proven inappropriate, although that is not to say a more complex system of multiple unit costs would not have worked better.
- Complexity—any flexibility system has to be sufficiently simple and transparent to ensure that the opportunities for gaming are limited and the monitoring system for the regulatory agency is not prohibitively expensive. For example, if there are multiple unit costs and detailed reporting and calculations are required to allow the regulator to assess the impact on revenues, which could be insignificant, then a flexibility system may not make sense.

How Should a Trigger System be Designed?

Triggers should:

- Be simple, clear, transparent and easily measurable—choose a small number of actions that act as the triggers and ensure that the opportunities for disagreement about whether the trigger has been met are very limited.
- Sufficient to have a real incentive impact—having incentives or penalties whose impact relative to the funding cost of the investment is insignificant are unlikely to have anything but a signaling effect.
- Levied in a way that is easy to calculate—such as an impact on price/revenue.

Should positive rather than negative triggers normally be employed? Because triggers make the most sense with large planned investments, it would seem to make sense to only use negative triggers—build the investment into the revenue requirement as per the ex-ante ex-post approach and then provide penalties if the investment is not undertaken. If triggers are used with less predictable investments then it may make sense to use incentives such that revenue is enhanced when the investment is undertaken.

Why would a trigger system be used in preference to one of the others—such as an interim determination or ex-post assessment? For negative triggers it is clear, these are a way of locking in the timing of investment and so removing some of the gaming options for an operator. Positive triggers are less clear. However, when an investment is known and can be costed but the timing is unclear, then a positive trigger system may be preferable to the more intrusive interim determination approach and creates a better environment for investment than the ex-post assessment systems.

What is an Ideal Logging-up System?

Logging-up systems should:

- Ensure revenue-neutrality by allowing funding costs to be covered.
- Have clear rules about how the ex-post assessment will be undertaken.
- Be applied normally only for small non-predictable investments, preferably for a limited set of areas (to limit the development of a "funding" mentality).

A logging-up system should be able to provide an operator with a degree of confidence about how small unforeseen investments will be handled. In most cases the cash flow implications of allowing logging-up to capture all unforeseen investments (small and large) or even all investment is such that this is not appropriate.

At What Level Should a Materiality Threshold be Set?

When thinking about some of the approaches it is important to set materiality thresholds to ensure that costly processes are avoided wherever possible. Consequently, when thinking about setting materiality thresholds following criteria should be considered:

- the cash flow implications (if the threshold involves moving from one regulatory approach to another like the logging-up to interim determination threshold)—these should be considered relative to the financial strength of the company since the regulator should have a concern about ensuring the viability of the industry;
- the expected direct and indirect costs of the regulatory approach—ensuring that only significant issues are addressed through the costly approaches like interim determinations and also that the limited time of the regulatory agency is not wasted dealing with trivial matters; and
- feasible ranges for cyclical or temporary movements in the cost elements over a price control period and the likelihood that these could self-correct within that period—temporary blips should not be sufficient to trigger materiality, rather structural shifts or new decisions imposing significant costs should be capable of crossing the threshold.

For example, in the Manila water and sewerage contracts there is a requirement for exchange rates to move by more than 2 percent before that is considered material, while the Buenos Aires water contract required a 7 percent movement in costs before being considered material.

When Should Pre-payment be Utilized?

Pre-payment has significant implications for existing consumers and so it is important to consider under what circumstances it is appropriate. These are likely to involve:

- The degree to which existing consumers will benefit from the investments—if there is some reason as to why existing consumers may benefit to a greater degree than would normally be expected, or could place a higher value on this service than future consumers then pre-payment would be justified.
- The cash flow implications of the investment—what would happen to prices and/or the sequencing of investment if the operator has to undertake the investment in the normal way on its balance sheet? If the investment would be delayed since access to finance would not be available or the cost of funding would become prohibitively expensive then this would provide a justification for pre-payment.
- The ability to unwind the pre-payment in the future—if this pre-payment is short-term, say between one price control period and the next, then would the majority of existing consumers be able to benefit from unwinding these pre-payments in the future price control period? If the majority of consumers would benefit then pre-payment could be justified.

Appendix: The Case Studies

No.	Country and sectors	Approaches utilized	Authors
1	Abu Dhabi, electricity and water distribution	▨ Logging-up (LU)	Aftab Raza (RSB)
2	Argentina (Buenos Aires), water and sewerage	▨ Ex-ante ex-post ▨ Ex-post prudency (or LU)	Martin Pardina (Macroenergia)
3	Argentina, electricity transmission	▨ Ex-post prudency ▨ Contracting-out	Martin Pardina (Macroenergia)
4	Australia, electricity transmission	▨ Ex-ante ex-post ▨ Ex-post prudency (or LU)	Eric Groom (World Bank)
5	Chile, electricity distribution	▨ Interim determination	Martin Pardina (Macroenergia)
6	Chile, water and sewerage	▨ Interim determination	Martin Pardina (Macroenergia)
7	England and Wales, water and sewerage	▨ Ex-ante ex-post ▨ Logging-up ▨ Interim determinations	Tony Ballance, Scott Reid, and Stuart King (Shaw Group)
8	England and Wales, electricity transmission	▨ Connection charging ▨ Error correction	Tony Ballance, Scott Reid, and Stuart King (Shaw Group)
9	Great Britain, gas distribution	▨ Pay-as-you-go	Ian Alexander and Katharina Gassner (World Bank)
10	India, electricity transmission	▨ Ex-post prudency ▨ Accelerated depreciation	Manish Agarwal and Siddharth Sen (PwC)
11	Philippines (Manila), water and sewerage	▨ Ex-ante ex-post ▨ Logging-up ▨ Interim determinations	Perry Rivera (Manila Water Co.)
12	Peru, electricity transmission	▨ Ex-post prudency ▨ Contracting-out	Martin Pardina (Macroenergia)
13	Scotland, water and sewerage	▨ Contracting-out	Tony Ballance, Scott Reid, and Stuart King (Shaw Group)
14	Ukraine, electricity	▨ Ex-post prudency	Yuri Kubrushko (IMEPower Investment Group)
15	UK, airports	▨ Triggers (negative)	Ian Alexander (World Bank)

Case Study 1: Electricity and Water Transmission and Distribution in Abu Dhabi

Regulatory instrument targeting investment uncertainty	Logging up and down
Industry concerned	Water and electricity—transmission and distribution
Ownership structure	All companies in the sector are wholly-owned by the government, except for Independent Water and Power Producers (IWPPs).
	The sector is characterized by a single-buyer model where the single-buyer purchases water and electricity from a number of generation and desalination companies (mostly IWPPs) for onward sale to the two distribution companies.
	There is a separate transmission and despatch company, the Abu Dhabi Transmission and Despatch Company (Transco), responsible for both water and electricity transmission with accounting separation between its water and electricity businesses. Further, there are two distribution companies, Abu Dhabi Distribution Company (ADDC) and Al Ain Distribution Company (AADC), each responsible for four separate businesses (with accounting separation) in their respective authorized areas: electricity distribution, electricity supply, water distribution and water supply. The terms of the licenses require preparation of audited separate accounts for each of the separate businesses.
Sector background	The sector is responsible for supply of potable water and electricity to the population of the Emirate of Abu Dhabi (more than 1.4m people over an area of approximately 67,340 square kilometers), the largest of the seven emirates of the United Area Emirates (UAE).
	Until 1998 a single vertically-integrated government department was responsible for all sector activities. Following the passage of Law No. 2 of 1998, the sector was unbundled, both horizontally and vertically, into a number of companies. The sector has a customer base of about 300,000 households, commercial, industrial and agricultural consumers with per capita consumption of water and electricity among the highest in the world. The sector has seen rapid growth in demand and capacity over the last few years, often with a two-digit annual growth rate. In 2003, the peak electricity and water demands were 4,134 MW and 400 MGD. The Law also established the Regulation and Supervision Bureau as the independent regulator for the sector and defines its duties and powers. All the sector companies are licensed by the Bureau.
	The natural monopoly parts of the industry, ie, Transco, and the two distribution companies, ADDC and AADC are subject to CPI-X price controls set by the regulator. In addition, the Abu Dhabi Water and Electricity Company (ADWEC), acting as single buyer for the sector faces controls regarding its procurement costs.
	There are separate controls for each of the electricity and water businesses of Transco, ADDC and AADC (and a single control for ADWEC). Distribution and supply activities of the

Case Study 1: Electricity and Water Transmission and Distribution in Abu Dhabi
   (*Continued*)

Regulatory instrument targeting investment uncertainty	Logging up and down
	two DISCOs are encompassed in the controls. That is, presently, there is no separation of controls between distribution and supply.
Form of regulatory regime	The first price controls (PC1) for the regulated transmission and distribution companies were put in effect from 1 January 1999 for three years and extended up to 2002. The price controls were reviewed in 2002 to set the second price controls (PC2) for the next three years (2003 to 2005). The new, or third, price controls (PC3) are therefore required for 2006 onwards.
Time frame of case study	PC1 and PC2 (1999 to 2005).
Rationale for using the approach	To date, the regulator's approach to the assessment and treatment of capex in the price controls has been essentially an ex-post one. While the PC1 controls were set assuming no capex during the PC1 period, the PC2 controls were set with some provisional capex allowances for both the PC1 and PC2 periods. In setting both the price controls the decision on firm capex allowances were deferred to the next price control reviews and receipt of reliable information on actual capex spent and following an assessment by the regulator of the capex spent against its established efficiency criteria.
	Little information was available to the regulator at the time of setting the PC1 controls regarding the regulated companies' future capex requirements. Only a figure for one year was submitted by Transco at the time and the figures of one of the two distribution companies had to be disregarded entirely because they were found incomplete. At the same time, an independent engineering consultancy, Merz and McLellan (M&M), had provided some estimates for the capex requirements.
	In view of the available information, and given the rapid demand growth the sector was facing, the regulator judged that the scope for errors in forecasting capex was very large. Thus, the following approach of complete logging up of capex expenditure was adopted: for the price control period 1999–2001, no provision for capex was made when calculating allowed revenues and the allowed costs of the Abu Dhabi companies therefore comprised only opex and the depreciation and return on initial capital. Actual but efficient capex spent was to be rolled forward into the subsequent price control period, appropriately capitalized, to be included in the opening 2003 regulatory asset base at the time of setting the PC2 controls.
	When assessing the merits of the approach, the regulator sought to satisfy itself that the proposed treatment would not result in an inappropriately low level of allowed revenue

(*Continued*)

Case Study 1: Electricity and Water Transmission and Distribution in Abu Dhabi
            (Continued)

Regulatory instrument targeting investment uncertainty	Logging up and down
	during the PC1 period, and would not result in large movements in unit prices between one control and the next. The regulator considered that excluding capex for the first three years would be justifiable as it would lower the allowed revenue on the one hand, but would on the other cause a decline in the regulatory asset base (RAB) which in turn would lead to lower required returns. However, the companies should be indifferent to this approach over a longer term in NPV terms since the future price controls would compensate the companies for their actual efficient capex with the foregone depreciation and return on capital along with the financing costs associated with such capex. In addition to the informational constraints, it appears likely that the following circumstances played a role in the logging up approach adopted by the Abu Dhabi regulatory agency: ▓ the network's systems were relatively young, and it was seen as unlikely that over the period of the price control there would be significant replacement expenditure; ▓ the transmission and distribution networks had received significant capex in the years before the first price control; and ▓ a recent investigation by technical consultants had pronounced the security standards in electricity as good; the standards in water were being looked into. In 2002 when setting the PC2 controls the regulator faced difficulties in accurately identifying the amount of capex actually undertaken during the PC1 period (1999 to 2002) due to the lack of audited data for that period. The regulator was also concerned with the uncertainties associated with the companies' projections of future capex for the PC2 period. Consequently, for the PC2 controls the regulator included as provisional allowances within its financial projections a proportion of the investment which the companies had undertaken since 1999, and a proportion of the investment which the companies planned to undertake until 2005. It was agreed that the regulator would review these provisional allowances following the receipt of reliable data from the companies on their actual capex and following an assessment of the actual capex against the regulator's efficiency criteria. This approach of allowing some provisional amounts of capex (for both past and future) investments was principally aimed at minimizing revenue volatility across the price control periods, and was thus preferred to the alternative of continuing to allow zero capex pending the receipt of audited data (as was done for PC1).
Scope of mechanism	All capex.

Case Study 1: Electricity and Water Transmission and Distribution in Abu Dhabi
(Continued)

Regulatory instrument targeting investment uncertainty	Logging up and down
Regulatory process	Described below.
Symmetry of mechanism	Symmetrical since it applies to all capex.
Description of mechanism and regulatory treatment of expenses	Upon introducing the capex logging up approach, the Abu Dhabi regulator stressed that evaluating capex on the basis of what was actually spent during the previous period should not be confused with pass-through of expenditure. He stressed that he would wish to be satisfied that capital expenditure had been properly incurred and that a reasonable and consistent approach had been adopted towards the capitalization of costs—carrying, or financing, costs associated with properly incurred capex would also be allowed. It was agreed at the 1999 review that actual CAPEX was to be added to the RAB at the 2002 review for the PC2 controls only if it met certain criteria: ▓ First that the expenditures were required to meet growth in customer demand or the relevant security standards. ▓ Second, the regulator would benchmark and market test actual expenditure to establish that they were efficiently procured. The same efficiency criteria was established at the 2002 review for the future assessment of PC1 and PC2 capex for which provisional allowances were made in the PC2 controls.
Degree of cost pass-through	As noted above, an assessment of the investment expenditure would be undertaken at the next review and then an amount to be passed-through would be determined. Broad principles were provided to the companies as to what would be construed as 'efficiently incurred' capex by the regulator.
Evidence of performance	At the PC review in 2002, the regulator proceeded in the following manner to account for past capex spend. Because of continued absence of audited data on past capex, the regulator made a *provisional* capex allowance. For AADC, the figures are based on reported levels of capex in 1999, which appeared the most reliable figures to the regulator. For Transco and ADDC, the figures have been set at 75% of the estimated capex submitted by the companies. It was agreed at the 2002 review that once audited data on actual 1999–2002 capex is received by the regulator, it will be reviewed against the efficiency criteria established by the regulator. Any difference between efficient past capex and the provisional assumptions made by the regulator will be reflected in an appropriate adjustment to the RAB at the 2005 review. It is interesting to note that a performance incentive scheme was introduced for each company under the PC2, to provide a stronger incentive for companies to improve

(Continued)

Case Study 1: Electricity and Water Transmission and Distribution in Abu Dhabi
          (*Continued*)

Regulatory instrument targeting investment uncertainty	Logging up and down
	their performance, in particular with regard to information disclosure. The two performance indicators selected for each business relate to timeliness of audited accounts and of audited price control returns, for which good (poor) performance will lead to an upward (downward) adjustment to allowed revenues via a correction term in the price control formula. The adjustment in any year will be capped at 2% of revenue in respect of 'own costs' (*i.e.,* excluding cost past through) in that year.
	The performance of the companies on preparation of audited information has recently improved. In response to the Performance Incentive Scheme, companies have provided the regulator with audited accounts and audited price control returns for 1999–2003.
	A comparison of the 1999 forecasts and the provisional capex allowance accorded to ADDC and AADC electricity businesses at the 2002 review highlights that the capex allowances were lower than the forecast capex for the PC1 (1999–2002) period. According to the 1999 forecasts, total capex spend for ADDC for the 4 year period was AED 1,805m; the actual allowance provisionally allowed by the regulator at the 2002 review is AED 1,284m. For AADC, the provisional allowance at the 2002 review was AED 755m for the period, compared to the 1999 forecast of AED 1,706m for the same period. In both cases the provisional allowances based on actual capex were significantly lower than the 1999 forecast.
	In contrast, in the case of Transco, over the PC1 period (1999–2002), the sum provisionally allowed by the regulator is AED 2,895m. The sum of forcast capex requirement by M&M in 1999 over the same period was AED 2,476m.
	The above comparisons tend to confirm the regulator's concerns about the robustness of the forecast capex in 1999.
Opportunity for gaming	Treatment of opex associated with the capex. Since there was a risk that capitalized costs would be written down (due to a lack of efficiency) some costs could be moved to opex and expensed immediately. No evidence of this type of gaming has been seen.
Primary information sources	"Second Consultation on the Water and Electricity Price Controls for Abu Dhabi Distribution Company and Al Ain Distribution Company," Regulation and Supervision Bureau, August 1999.
	"Second Consultation on the Water and Electricity Price Controls for Abu Dhabi Transmission and Despatch Company," Regulation and Supervision Bureau, July 1999.
	"2002 Price Controls Review—Final Proposals for PC2," Regulation and Supervision Bureau, November 2002.

Case Study 2: Argentina—Buenos Aires Water and Sewerage

Regulatory instrument targeting investment uncertainty	Ex ante, ex post approach
Industry concerned	Buenos Aires water and sewerage company
Ownership structure	In 1993 the Argentine government concessioned water and sewerage in Buenos Aires city and part of the metropolitan area (the public company was transferred to Lyonnaise des Eaux-Dumez). The area of the concession contained 9 million persons, where 6 million were connected to the water grid and 5 million to sewerage (covering 70% and 58% respectively). At the moment of the concession, the water grid covered 11.000 kilometers and sewerage 7.000 kilometers. The public company, Obras Sanitarias de la Nación (OSN), was producing 3,7 million cubic meters per day. The concession was auctioned for 30 years.
Sector background	Regulatory Entity: "Ente Triparito de Obras y Servicios Sanitarios" (ETOSS). The functions and obligations of ETOSS are: ■ enforce the contract and the regulatory framework ■ approve the regulatory norms for the dealings with and complaints by users to be proposed by the concessionaire ■ request from concessionaire the data required to conduct its supervision and ensure the confidentiality of the information provided ■ publicize the expansion plans, service improvements plans and the tariffs ■ monitor the compliance of the concessionaire of the various plans ■ record the complaints by users on service and tariff problems ■ make decisions on complaints and other conflicts based on careful examination of facts ■ assess and endorse or reject the request for revisions on tariffs ■ enforce commitments and obligations by concessionaire on investment and maintenance ■ intervene in decision on renegotiation of contract ■ apply sanctions on concessionaire as specified in the contract and return the revenue from penalties to users as additional investment or tariff reductions to be specified in bills ■ request the assistance of the executive power when the actions of the concessionaire impose a threat on the health of the population.
Form of regulatory regime	Type of regulation: ■ cost plus ■ initial tariff level set in the privatization process

(*Continued*)

Case Study 2: Argentina—Buenos Aires Water and Sewerage (*Continued*)

Regulatory instrument targeting investment uncertainty	Ex ante, ex post approach
	▨ trigger rule for changes based on a known cost structure
	Quality requirements:
	▨ water quality levels are spelled out
	▨ no quality norms with respect to service cuts or water pressure levels
	Investments requirements:
	▨ include improvement and expansion plans as part of the contract
	▨ investment have to be bid out
	▨ timing requirements for the investment program, but subject to renegotiation.
Time frame of case study	Renegotiation of the five year period, 1993 to 1998.
Rationale for using the approach	Although the divergence of the investments goals can be accepted by the regulator ex post, under no circumstance could this imply an economic-financial benefit for the concessionaire. For this reason, the cash flow is adjusted to take into account divergences between what was planned and what really happened (beside the penalties that the regulator can impose for not reaching the established goals).
Scope of mechanism	The mechanism covers all capex and opex.
Regulatory process	To fix the tariff for the next five year period, the regulator uses the concept of "Exposición Financiera Neta Quinquenal" (EFNQ)—this can be translated as five year net financial exposure. The EFNQ is designed to reflect the degree of performance achieved by the concessionaire in the complying with the goals of the "Plan de Mejoras y Expansion del Servicio" (PMES)—the Improvements and Service Expansion Plan. In this sense, the EFNQ is determined by correcting the planned cash flows for each of the five years by the deviations occurred from those goals. In order to do these, the mechanism "ex ante—ex post" of validating of investments considers:
	(1) Committed but not realized investments, when the undoing was motivated by circumstances under the concessionaire's responsibility.
	(2) Realized investments that, even that were not included in the five years investment plan, they qualify as useful and convenient for the development of the concession (of course, including the associated opex of these investments). The regulator, ex post, decides which investments are "useful" or "convenient".
	(3) The effect over income and opex, capex and taxes caused by force majeure or circumstances not imputable to the concessionaire and that are not receipted by any passed five years tariff revisions.

Case Study 2: Argentina—Buenos Aires Water and Sewerage (*Continued*)

Regulatory instrument targeting investment uncertainty	Ex ante, ex post approach
	Once the cash flows are corrected in the way just described, they are capitalized by the cost of capital determined by five year period up to the year of the tariff review. So, the EFNQ is:
	$$EFNQ_m = \sum_{\gamma=1}^{5} FFN_\gamma \cdot (1 + r_m)^{6-\gamma}$$
	Where:
	FFN_γ is the net planned cash flow corrected for the year γ. r_m is the cost of capital for fixed for the five year period. The tariffs for the next five year period are fixed using as a reference the EFNQ. For example, for the five-year period under analysis (1993–1998) the EFNQ was of $823.345 million.
Symmetry of mechanism	Symmetric (the mechanism of ex ante ex post recognition of expenses is applied to capex and opex, without existing, in principle, exceptions).
Description of mechanism and regulatory treatment of expenses	Some examples of how the ex ante—ex post mechanism (of recognition of investments) was applied for the five-year period under analysis (1993–1994):
	(1) The regulator approved some investments using an efficiency criterion. For example, the concessionaire had made expenses in order to determine constructed squared meters and to make a list of clients—the "Relevamiento Catastral y Padrón de clientes." This item was not included on the allow capex and opex for the period. The efficiency criterion here consisted in studying if the incorporation of these expenses generated more revenue than costs (considering both, capex and opex). In this case, ETOSS found that validating this expenses was "efficient" and, therefore, decided to recognized them (this meant an augmentation of expenses by $45 million—between capex and opex).
	(2) Another criteria used by ETOSS in order to approve, ex post increments of the planned investments was to see if that investments lead to minor tariff changes for the next five year period (remembered that this adjustments of ex ante investments affects the EFNQ and this, in turn, affect the tariffs of the next period). For example, this criterion was used to evaluate the "voluntary retirement plan"—used by the operator to reduce the excess labor inherited with the concession. ETOSS, using this reasoning, approved this expenses. So, planned expenses in this item of $37 million, ex post, passed to $70 million.
Degree of cost pass-through	The investments, ex ante, were (in $ millions): year 1: Evidence of performance $101.5; year 2:$242.83; year 3:$343.57; year 4:$315.87; year 5:$367.47.

(*Continued*)

Case Study 2: Argentina—Buenos Aires Water and Sewerage (*Continued*)

Regulatory instrument targeting investment uncertainty	Ex ante, ex post approach
	The investments, ex post, were of (in million): year 1: $195.73; year 2: $244.45; year 3: $213.3; year 4: $139.75; year 5: $239.74.
	The differences between year 2 and 5 are explained by changes in the PMES. For example, in sewerage, the offered investment was of $103.3 million for year 3 while the investment executed for that year was $1.3 (for year 4 there is a similar difference of about $103.24 million).

Case Study 3: Argentine Electricity Transmission

Regulatory instrument targeting investment uncertainty	Contracting-out and logging-up
Industry concerned	Argentine transmission sector
Ownership structure	A basic law governing the sector was passed by Congress in December 1991 and went into effect in January 1992. The main thermal plants, distribution, and transmission companies owned by the national government were sold to the private sector through competitive bidding in 1992 and 1993, and most of the national government's hydro plants were concesioned the following year. The only major facilities that remained in the national government's hands were two nuclear plants and two large hydro dams that had been developed cooperatively with the governments of Uruguay and Paraguay. The provinces were encouraged to privatize their distribution companies and most did in the 1990s. From a total of eight transmission companies, between 1992 and 1995, six of them were privatized. The other two companies are owned by regional governments.
Sector background	Although there are eight transmission companies, the most important is Transener S.A., which was responsible for maintaining and operating the high-voltage transmission grid that connected major generating and consuming regions of the country. Transener's system consisted of nearly 7000 kilometers of 500 kV lines and covered the entire country except the Patagonia region, which was not connected to the national grid. There were six regional transmission companies with lines of 220 kV or less. One regional company served Patagonia and the other five filled in the network in areas served by Transener. The eight company was a specialized independent company that operated an 800 kilometer 500-kV line connecting the government-owned Yacyretá dam with Buenos Aires region.
Form of regulatory regime	The price system for transmission of electricity is a hybrid that has elements of price cap, revenue caps and clauses of investments in quality. The principal component of revenue comes from a fix sum whose calculation is based in the expected value of the energy loses (this estimation is made by Cammesa and subject to ENRE's approval in each tariff review). In the company's point of view this fixed sum functions as a revenue cap that endures for five years (up to the next tariff revision). Other revenues come from connection charges (that individually are subject to a price cap), other complementary charges and eventually a premium for high availability of the lines (which is determined administratively). On the cost side, there are penalties for unavailability and other quality elements.
Regulation	ENRE (Ente Nacional Regulador de Electricidad) regulated the three distribution companies and six transmission companies that had concessions from the national government.

(*Continued*)

Case Study 3: Argentine Electricity Transmission (*Continued*)

Regulatory instrument targeting investment uncertainty	Contracting-out and logging-up
	One of ENRE's main responsibilities was to set the tariffs and administer a system of penalties and bonuses designed to control quality. ENRE's decisions could be overruled, however, by the Minister of the Economy and Energy. A nonprofit company, CAMMESA, coordinates the dispatch of power plants to insure that the supply and the demand were constantly in balance and that the plants that had the lower costs to supply power were dispatched first.
Time frame of case study	1998 Transener's tariff review (covering the period 1993 to 1998).
Scope of mechanism	Capex and Opex.
Regulatory process for deciding grid expansions	There are three different methodologies:

- **Minor improvements.** For improvements that cost less than $2 million. In such cases, Transener would build and maintain the improvements and ENRE would determine who would pay.

- **Contract between parties.** For improvements that involved only one or a few Transener customers, such as a short extension to connect a new wholesale customer to Transener's high-voltage lines. In such cases, Transener would usually build and maintain the facility with the customers involved reimbursing Transener for its costs. The customers were expected to negotiate an agreement with Transener. ENRE had to review the agreement to make sure that the improvement served the public interest and that Transener was not abusing its monopoly position in the negotiations. As part of its review, ENRE was required to hold public hearings on the proposed agreement.

- **Open competition.** For major new lines that would be used by many parties. ENRE would investigate a new line only if generators, distributors, and large industrial consumers who were thought to receive at least 30 percent of the benefit from the line requested. In such cases, ENRE would estimate the costs of the line, identify the beneficiaries more carefully, and hold a public hearing. Unless parties who received at least 30 percent of the benefit objected at the hearing, ENRE would then authorize the proponents of the project to conduct a competition for a new concession to construct, operate and maintain (COM) the new line. The concessionaire would recover its construction through an annual fee to be charged for the first 15 years, and its operating and maintenance costs through a tariff schedule that was similar to Transener's. The concession would be awarded to the bidder offering the lowest annual construction fee. The users of the line would pay the annual fee, with their individual shares being proportional to the degree to which they were thought to be benefit from the line.

Case Study 3: Argentine Electricity Transmission (*Continued*)

Regulatory instrument targeting investment uncertainty	Contracting-out and logging-up
	In practice there is also a **fourth method**. Whereas the above new facilities are available for open access along with existing facilities, Article 31 of the Act enables the Secretary of Energy to authorize a generator, distributor or large user to construct a transmission line at its own cost and for its own use—resolution SE 179/1998 issued 8 May 1998 clarified and liberalized the conditions under which such authority would be granted.
	This policy has operated since the privatization of the power sector, essentially since 1993. In principle it still applies, although the freezing of electricity tariffs in February 2002 following the crisis and devaluation of the peso has essentially precluded normal regulatory processes, and much new investment is now widely seen as too risky.
	Nonetheless, there have been about eight years of experience with the Public Contest and other methods. However, under 10% by number of the expansion projects (16) were financed by the Public Contest method. A quarter (45) were financed by Contract between Parties. Over 60% (118) were Minor expansions (of these, 113 were Minor Expansions by Contract between Parties and 5 were Other Minor Expansions. There was no difference in the average value of these two sub-categories). The remaining 4% (7) proceeded under Article 31. However, the Public Contest expansions were by far the biggest, accounting for two-thirds of the expansions by value ($538m). Contract between Parties accounted for a quarter ($217m). Minor expansions accounted for 8% in total ($70m). Article 31 expansions were 1.5 per cent by value ($12m).This means that the average sizes of expansions were Public Contest $34m, Contract between Parties $5m, Article 31 $1.7m and Minor expansions $0.6m.
	With a small number of projects of differing sizes, overall averages can be misleading. ENRE reports that, of the nine largest projects, five were built using the Public Contest method and four used Contracts between Parties. We may calculate that the four largest Public Contest projects had a total cost of $479 m. This means that the remaining 12 Public Contest projects totalled $60m, an average of $5m each. In other words, apart from the four largest projects, the 12 remaining Public Contest projects had the same average size as the 45 projects by Contract Between Parties.
Symmetry of mechanism	Symmetric.
Description of mechanism and regulatory treatment of expenses	In the tariff review, four aspects were discussed between interest parties:
	(1) **Unregulated activities**. Transener was involved in other activities besides operating and maintenance the existing

---

Case Study 3: Argentine Electricity Transmission (*Continued*)

Regulatory instrument targeting investment uncertainty	Contracting-out and Logging-up

high-voltage grid. These activities included Transba, the fourth Comahue-Buenos Aires line, minor expansions of the existing grid that Transener was undertaking on behalf of specific customers, and related activities it was developing, such as the use of its rights of way and towers for telecoms lines and equipment. Transener had excluded from its tariff calculation the costs and revenues of those activities were most readily separable, notably Transba and the fourth line. But for other activities whose costs were harder to isolate, Transener proposed not to try to separate them but instead to credit the regulated activity with some of the unregulated revenue. This methodology was considered very controversial and unclear.

(2) **Capital base**. Based on a document submitted by the National Bank of Argentina prior to the privatization, ENRE fixed the asset base in $275 million—this value was not know at the moment of privatization and there were strict legal provisions about not disclosing the valuation to the bidders. The valuation was done only because the government was required by law to do it before the sale. In this way, ENRE, rejected Transener's proposal to consider a value of $406 million (this was the amount offered by Transener for the concession).

On the side of investments, Transener requested to ENRE the recognition of: $21.81 for the year 1994, $18.69 for 1995, $8.51 for 1996, $11.47 for 1997 and $12.60 for 1998. However, ENRE did not take into account those quantities. On the contrary, the regulator established a formula to calculate them by taking the difference between the realized net investment (however, here ENRE did not recognize all the investments declared by Transener, rather it readjusted them claiming that they were over estimated)[35] and those nets investments estimated by National Bank of Argentina.[36] Also, given that an important fraction of realized investments over the period were part of unregulated activities, ENRE considered only 85% of them. Thus, this implies that recognized investments by the regulator were: 1994:$4.5; 1995:$2.7; 1996:$5.1; 1997:$6.3; and 1998:$6.1.[37]

(3) **Future Investments**. By law, Transener does not have the obligation to expand the grid, its commitment is only to maintain the assets in order to avoid penalties

---

35. The net investments considered by ENRE after the mentioned readjustment were (in millions): 1994:$15,97; 1995:$9,8; 1996:$–1.34; 1997:$4,28; 1998:$2,8 (*source:* ENRE).

36. Investments established in the document of the National Bank of Argentina were: 1994:$18.1; 1995:$2.7; 1996:$5.1; 1997:$6.3; 1998:$6.1 (*source:* ENRE).

37. In order to clarify, the formula applied by ENRE, for example for 1994 was: 15.97*0.85–18.1 (*source:* Resolución 1650/99, ENRE).

Case Study 3: Argentine Electricity Transmission (*Continued*)

Regulatory instrument targeting investment uncertainty	Contracting-out and Logging-up
	derived from not reaching the service quality standards. Transener manifested that net investments for the next five-year period were (in millions): for 1999: $6.69; 2000: $8.94; 2001: $13.04; 2002: $12.9; and 2003: $11.06. However, ENRE estimated net investments for that period were: 1999: $5.85; 2000: $10.47; 2001: $11.44; 2002: $15.78; 2003: $15.05.
Primary information sources	ENRE 2002 Annual Report.

Case Study 4: Electricity transmission in Australia

Regulatory instrument targeting investment uncertainty	Current: ex-post prudency test Proposed: firm ex ante cap
Industry concerned	Electricity transmission
Ownership structure	ACCC regulates 6 regionally-based transmission companies—including EnergyAustralia which is predominantly a distribution network company and retailer but which also owns $629 m in transmission assets (approximately 11.6% of its total asset base) that are regulated by the ACCC. Access to its distribution network services is regulated by IPART. Two are privately owned and the remainder (including TransGrid (TG)) are state government owned.
Sector background	The transcos were established in the second half of the 1990's initial price paths set by state government's or state-based regulators. The states gradually transferred responsibility for transmission regulation to the ACCC (the national regulator). The ACCC has commenced its second round of price reviews with price resets for TG and EnergyAustralia (EA). Together TG and EA have a regulatory asset base (RAB) of $A3.55 billion and spent $A1.33 billion in the 5 years to 2004, which was almost 40% above the allowance for capex incorporated in the price path to 2004.
Form of regulatory regime	5 year revenue cap set by ACCC.
Time frame of case study	Initial price control period 1999–2004 (end-June financial years) Reset for 2004–2009 underway. The draft report has been issued.
Rationale for using the approach	*Current:* The current approach was adopted to provide strong incentives for the utility to optimize their capex spending. If the actual capex was less than the forecast the utility would retain the benefits (ie the depreciation and return on the capex not spent) for 5 years under the rolling incentive mechanism. The converse applied to expenditure above the forecast capex. The ACCC strengthened the incentive to avoid inefficient investment or inefficient use of existing assets by retaining the option of writing down the value of new or existing assets where they were deemed imprudent or inefficiently utilized. *Proposed:* The ACCC proposes changing to a firm ex ante cap to reduce investment risk and regulatory "intrusiveness." The ACCC considers that the risk of subsequent optimization (stranding) of assets creates too much uncertainty for investors and may discourage necessary investment. It was also concerned that the ex post review required an intrusive and burdensome review of individual projects. Finally, it has been difficult to determine the extent of asset write-down if a project is considered imprudent.
Scope of mechanism	*Current:* The current mechanism covers all assets.

Case Study 4: Electricity transmission in Australia (*Continued*)

Regulatory instrument targeting investment uncertainty	Current: ex-post prudency test Proposed: firm ex ante cap
	Proposed:
	The ACCC is considering whether a firm ex ante cap should cover all assets. It has raised the options of excluding capex on inter-regional links, large network projects or augmentation projects.
	In each case the projects considered for exclusion may be less predictable but, if excluded, an individual review of each project would be required. The ACCC is particularly concerned about the complexities and distortions that could result from excluding large projects and augmentation projects.
Regulatory process	ACCC's reviews are conducted under the national electricity laws and the National Electricity Code (NEC). The processes include public submissions from utilities and stakeholders, various public fora and publication of a draft report prior to the final report. The NEC obliges the ACCC to fully explain its decisions. Appeals are to the Federal Court or High Court under administrative law.
	For the ex ante review at the start of a regulatory period:
	▓ The utility submits a detailed capex program
	▓ The ACCC reviews this to determine whether the proposed expenditures are necessary and efficient. The ACCC generally commissions an independent expert assessment.
	▓ The ACCC builds the capex path it determines appropriate into the cost building blocks for setting the revenue cap.
	For the ex post review at the end of the regulatory period:
	▓ The utility reports its past capex in the format requested by the ACCC
	▓ The ACCC reviews this capex to test whether the expenditure was prudent. As part of this the ACCC compares actual expenditure against forecast. Projects included in the forecast program and delivered below expected cost are subject to less scrutiny. A much higher standard of prudency is set for large projects delivered at higher-than-forecast costs. The ACCC commissions assessments from an independent expert to assist it.
	▓ Capex considered prudent is included in the RAB.
Symmetry of mechanism	*Current:*
	In principle the current incentive mechanism for variation in actual and forecast capex can be applied symmetrically to over and underspending. However, sanctions for underperformance will in theory exceed rewards for overperformance because:
	▓ The test sets 'best practice' as the benchmark rather than say average or better than average performance.

Case Study 4: Electricity transmission in Australia (*Continued*)

Regulatory instrument targeting investment uncertainty	Current: ex-post prudency test Proposed: firm ex ante cap
	▓ Stranding of investment not deemed prudent provides an an ongoing sanction on poor performance whereas the benefits for better performance are temporary.
	Proposed:
	The proposed mechanism is asymmetrical. The utility would lose the entire return of and on expenditure in excess of the ex ante cap unless it was separately approved under a one-off review. It would retain the initial benefits of the return on and of the ex ante capex cap not spent. But this benefit would be phased out over the subsequent regulatory period.
Description of mechanism and regulatory treatment of expenses	*Current:* Under the current approach:[38]
	▓ At the start of the regulatory period the ACCC includes an allowance for Capex in the revenue base sufficient to enable the utility to efficiently meet its service obligations.
	▓ At the end of the regulatory period the ACCC assesses the prudency of the capital expenditure, expecially where actual costs exceed forecast costs.
	▓ Capital expenditure considered prudent is rolled into the initial RAB for the next regulatory period.
	▓ A quality of service factor is included in the revenue cap to reduce the incentives to reduce capex at the expense of a decline in service standards.
	The ex post prudency test comprises three questions:
	▓ was there a justifiable need for the project?
	▓ was the proposal the most efficient means of meeting that need?
	▓ was the proposed solution built/delivered efficiently?
	During the regulatory period the utility retains the benefit of any reductions in capex cost relative to forecast. Conversely it does not earn a return of or on any expenditure above the forecast. These benefits and losses are phased out (*i.e.* shared with customers) over the next regulatory period.
	Any expenditure that is above forecast expenditure but deemed prudent is rolled into the asset base for the start of the next regulatory period at its undepreciated value plus an allowance for the foregone return—this can be achieved by rolling forward the RAB by deducting depreciation based

---

38. In Victoria the transmission planning function is undertaken by Vencorp, the market administrator. SPI Powernet (a privately-owned Transco) does not determine augmentation needs and Vencorp has no financial interest in increasing projected capex or pursing network augmentation rather than other options. Hence the need for prudency reviews, their significance and the risks they create are greatly reduced.

Case Study 4: Electricity transmission in Australia (*Continued*)

Regulatory instrument targeting investment uncertainty	Current: ex-post prudency test Proposed: firm ex ante cap
	on forecast capex at the start of the regulatory period rather than depreciation based on actual capex. This means that the depreciation and return on that expenditure in the regulatory period in which it was incurred is deferred not foregone entirely.
	Transmission augmentations are also subject to a separate ex-ante regulatory test under the National Electricity Code to determine whether the project is of net benefit. While this is not necessarily linked to the ex-post prudency review, the ACCC has placed significant weight on the regulatory test in its prudency reviews.
	Proposed:
	The utility will propose a 5 year price cap which the ACCC would assess. The ACCC would then establish a firm cap at the start of each regulatory control period as a profile of expenditure rather than as a specified list of projects and expected costs.
	The choice and timing of projects actually undertaken would be a matter for the utility. Provided that its total capex is less than the ex-ante cap the ACCC will not assess the prudency of the projects and the spending will be rolled into the RAB. Expenditure above the ex ante cap would be excluded from the RAB.
	Issues still to be addressed are the approaches for setting the ex ante cap and sharing the benefits of better performance between the utility and customers. Options for setting the cap include a detailed project-by-project review similar to OfWat's approach, benchmarks based on historical trends or cost and efficiency models of the sector. 'Off-ramps' may be provided for the reconsideration of the ex ante cap in extraordinary circumstances (yet to be defined).
Degree of cost pass-through	*Current:*
	Cost pass-through is subject to ex-post prudency review.
	TG spent $289m (32%) more than expected in 1999–2004. The prudency review resulted in the exclusion of $127m from the asset base. Optimisation of an existing 500kV line to 330kV accounted for $70m of this. Of the remainder the major component was a $44m reduction from the CBD augmentation. This was the largest single project undertaken by TG. Originally estimated to cost $143m, it is now forecast to cost $276m. At this cost other options were available that could have met the immediate requirements more cheaply and allowed deferral of the project. The ACCC noted that the extent of the write down was a matter of judgment and chose to write down the expenditure by $44m. This equates to the foregoing of any return during the period of construction (or the exclusion of capitalized interest during construction).

Case Study 4: Electricity transmission in Australia (*Continued*)

Regulatory instrument targeting investment uncertainty	Current: ex-post prudency test Proposed: firm ex ante cap
	Proposed: Costs up to the ex ante cap will be passed through with certainty. Costs above that would only be passed through if the project had been subject to separate, detailed, ex ante review.
Evidence of performance	Contrary to expectations, given the incentives under the current approach, actual capex has substantially exceeded forecast capex. It is not clear if this reflects shortcomings of the current mechanism or other factors such as the weaker efficiency incentives under government ownership.
Opportunity for gaming	In principle current mechanism provides a strong incentive to overstate forecast capex. This will continue under the proposed mechanism.
Primary information sources	ACCC, Review of the Draft Statement of Principles for the Regulation of Transmission Revenues—Capital Expenditure Framework, March 2004. ACCC, NSW and ACT Transmission Network revenue Caps—TransGrid and EA Reports, April 2004.

Case Study 5: Water and Sewerage in Chile

Regulatory instrument targeting investment uncertainty	Extraordinary tariffs revisions in the efficient firm model
Industry concerned	Chile water and sewerage companies
Ownership structure	The public sector maintains a strong presence in the sector although the share of private firms has increased recently. In December 2002 there were 12 private firms (which represented 77.5% of the market), 6 firms in the hands of COFRO[39] (with 16% of the market) and 19 firms own by the municipalities (4.5% of the market).
Sector background	Economic regulation for all water and sewerage companies is the responsibility of SISS (Superintendence of Sanitary Services). In 1994 the average rate of return on assets water companies was 6.2%, with the profitability of individual firms ranging between −4.5% and 13.2%. In 1998 was on average of 7 percent and for 2003, 8%.[40]
	Average tariff $/cubic meter ($ Dec. 2003):304.5 in 1997; 1998:303.4; 1999:309.9; 2000: 345.6; 2001: 368.2; 2002:431, finally for 2003, 464. Average tariff ($/cubic meter/client/month):7.418 in 1998; 1999:7.244; 2000:8.070; 2001:8.358; 2002:9.167.
	Investment data: between 1995 and 1998 the amount of investment (both in the sewage system, potable water and wastewater treatment) rise to M$473119 (that is US$1001 million—in 1998 values). Between 1999 and 2002 a similar amount was invested.

(Continued)

---

39. The COFRO ("Cooperación de fomento a la producción") is an organism of the Chilean state in charged of promoting the development of the national productive sector. By this organism the state participates in the sector owning equity of different firms (COFRO is a minor partner in 7 privatized firms).

40. Data

Firms	1988	1989	1990	1991	1992	1993	1994	1995	1998	1999	2000	2001	2002	2003
Rate of return on assets														
Public—CORFO	−1.4	−1.6	−1.1	−0.2	0.9	3.4	5.1	5.9	7	5.3	7.5	7.1	7.8	8
Private	−0.1	13.1	3.9	1.6	4	6.5	7.2	9.9						
Return on equity														
									6.5	2.9	7.4	8.6	9.8	12.1
Leverage (debt/equity)														
									28.5	25.9	32.2	46.8	59.6	120.6

Source: the "Informe de Gestión del Sector Sanitario," published by SISS (www.siss.cl).

Case Study 5: Water and Sewerage in Chile (*Continued*)

Regulatory instrument targeting investment uncertainty	Extraordinary tariffs revisions in the efficient firm model
Form of regulatory regime	*Tariffs calculation*

The regulation of tariffs is based on an ideal efficient firm.[41] Tariffs are fixed for five years. The efficient firm is defined as that one that operates at a minimum cost with the best technology available at that moment and complies with the service quality standards, adapted to the geographical conditions serving the demand of each area of service. Each stage of water/sanitation service is priced (capitation of untreated water, production of potable water and its distribution, collection of wastewater and disposal thereof[42]). Price-setting is done per firm and each pricing area corresponds to a system—a "system" consists of installations in the different stages of the sanitation service that can physically interact, and which should be jointly optimized to minimize the long-run costs of providing the service. The aim of defining a system is to optimize the network of the efficient firm so as to satisfy projected demand at minimum cost. *Efficient tariffs* are derived from the *incremental costs of development*: a value equivalent to a constant price per unit, that applied to a projected incremental demand, generates the required revenues to cover the efficient incremental costs of exploitation and the investment of a optimized expansion plan consistent with a zero net present value (article 4 of DFL 70, the "Sanitary Service's Tariffs Law"—and article 15 of D.S. MINECON N° 453, this "Supreme Decree number 453 of the Ministry of Economic, Foment and Reconstruction" of 1990, is the decree that regulates the "Sanitary Service's Tariffs Law").

To define what parameters will determine the efficient firm, both, the company and the regulator, participate in this process: A year before the new tariffs enter into force, the regulator (SISS) publishes the principles features of the study of a "model firm" (this study has the target to determine the efficient tariffs and the final tariffs for the next five-year-period). After a consultation period, the final base of the study is published. Over these final terms of reference, both the regulator and the firm develop simultaneously a study of the "model firm". Not later than five month before the new tariffs enter into force, the regulator and the firm exchange their final studies. The firm has a period of 30 days to present objections. After there is a 15-days period in order to negotiate the differences and to establish agreed tariffs. If there is

---

41. This means that the values and parameters that are considered to calculate the incremental costs of development, the total costs, and the efficient tariffs are not those of the real firm; on the contrary, a fictitious firm is contemplated (called the "model firm"). In other words, the criteria of the efficient firm respond to this question: If we could rethink the entire firm again, how we will redesign the firm in order to satisfy efficiently the demand?

42. The Ministry of Economic Affairs also establishes what can be charged for other services such as disconnection and reconnection of users in arrears, maintenance of public and private standpipes, direct control of liquid industrial waste (LIW) and a review of engineering projects for LIW treatment systems.

Case Study 5: Water and Sewerage in Chile (*Continued*)

Regulatory instrument targeting investment uncertainty	Extraordinary tariffs revisions in the efficient firm model
	no agreement, the Expert Commission intervenes. The Commission is formed by three members (one elected by the regulator, one by the firm and the third is elected from a list of three experts previously selected). The Commission has a month to determine the final tariffs. It has to support one of the two positions, and it is not possible to take middle positions.

This tariffs study starts with a demand estimation for the next 15 years (for the future it is assumed that the demand does not grow any more), differentiating between month of high consume of month of low consume.

If no expansion plans are considered, the *efficient tariffs are derived from* the long run marginal costs in a similar way (for more details see article 25 of D.S. MINECON N° 453). The cost of capital used is equal to the average internal rate of return offered by Chilean Central Bank in its domestic currency instruments with a term equal or over eight years, plus a risk premium that has to be between 3% and 3.5%. On the other hand, the cost of capital can be inferior to 7% (article 5 of DFL 70).

The sustainability problem. Calculated in this way, the efficient tariffs, do not guarantee the recover of the long run average costs. To solve this problem of sustainability, some kind of compensation has to be recognized. This compensation emerges from the difference between the annual revenue obtained from applying the efficient tariffs to the actualized annual demand for the tariffs revision period and the *total long run cost* derived from satisfying that demand. The concept of total long run costs is defined in detail in article 24 of D.S. MINECON N° 453—is the constant annual value required to cover the efficient cost of exploitation and investments of a optimized reposition plan. In consequence, the total long cost calculation considers the design of an efficient firm that initiates operations (accomplishes needed investments—taking into account an optimal path of growth and runs into exploitation expenses) earning a revenue compatible with a net present value equal to zero from the optimized reposition plan—considering all the demand and not only the incremental demand as in the case of the cost of development. If there is no difference between those concepts, efficient tariffs are accepted, otherwise they are readjusted to guarantee the equality (for more details see article 35 of D.S. MINECON N° 453). Finally, the efficient or the readjusted tariffs are indexed.

Article 35 suggests that the efficient tariffs (T_i^e)—for the different fix charges and prices have to be adjusted by a common factor to calculate the final tariffs (T_i):

$$T_i = T_i^e \cdot \lambda$$

$$\lambda = \frac{Total\ Costs}{Revenues}$$

(*Continued*)

Case Study 5: Water and Sewerage in Chile (*Continued*)

Regulatory instrument targeting investment uncertainty	Extraordinary tariffs revisions in the efficient firm model

This formula does not appear in the law (it only reflects the spirit of the law—see Andrés Gómez-Lobo and Miguel Vargas; "La regulación de las empresas sanitarias en Chile: una revisión del caso de EMOS y una propuesta de reforma regulatoria"; unpublished; 2002).

The treat of investments in the efficient firm model

The use of the efficient firm model implies considering only those investments that the efficient company would do (thus, the regulator, directly, does not recognize those investments that diverge from the efficient ones -that were planned in the final tariffs study). On this circumstances, the occurrence of exogenous facts that compel the company to do higher (or lower) investments that the efficient firm wouldn't do, triggers the mechanism of extraordinary tariffs review (only if, as explained, both the regulator and firm, agree to do this review). This mechanism tries to adjust the investments by the new conditions occurred (otherwise, if the company makes the investments without asking for a change of the parameters that defines the efficient firm, ex post, the regulator will not take into consideration those higher investments). Afterwards, some case studies of extraordinary reviews are explained.

The Development Plans[43]

It was noted that efficient tariffs are derived from the concept of incremental costs of development (ICD). Also, it was explained that the ICD is determined by the incremental efficient cost of exploitation and investment of an optimized expansion project (for an incremental demand projected over 15 years). These (optimized) projects, known as *Development Plans*, are agreed between the SISS and the concessionaries (see article 14 of the DFL MOP N° 382/88) and their objective is to fix a compromise about how the firms will manage to maintain the continuity and quality of the service and to expand installations in order to cover the projected demand (in a broad sense, to establish *solutions*—this is the idea that the legislation uses for satisfying that expected demand). On the other hand, investment plans for a period of 15 years have to be exposed in the *Development Programs* (the Development Programs are part of de Development Plans and show how the firms will materializes their compromised *solutions* to cover the projected demand specified in the them). Is important to say that SISS has the faculty to reject them. In each year the concessionaries have to

---

43. The norms that rule this aspect of the Chilean model are, basically: the "Ley General de Servicios Sanitarios" (el DFL MOP N° 382/88), the D.S. MOP N° 121 and the law N° 18.902.

Case Study 5: Water and Sewerage in Chile (*Continued*)

Regulatory instrument targeting investment uncertainty	Extraordinary tariffs revisions in the efficient firm model
	establish (in what is called "*The Annual Chronogram of Infrastructures*") the sums of investment, the infrastructure to build (or the percentage of infrastructure that will be executed on that year) that were compromised in the Development Programs and the day, in that year, in which each infrastructure will start to operate.

Annually the SISS has to control the execution of the Annual Chronogram of Infrastructures concessionaries. The enforcement of the obligations compromised by the firms in that Chronogram is considered in the legislation by giving to SISS's the faculty to fix monetary penalties every year (see article 55 of the DFL MOP N° 382/88). The Law N° 18902, in the article 11, specifies the penalties that have to be charged to those firms: "51 to 10000 of *Tributary Units* per year (known as UTA)…".[44] It is important to say that the penalties are imposed when firms do not accomplish with the construction of the compromised infrastructure in that year (that is, SISS does not make a monetary control of investment, but a physic check). The concessionaries have the possibility to appeal to the Justice.

Number and sums of penalties fixed by the SISS:

Item/Year	1999	2000	2001	2002
Number of penalties	10	3	5	1
US$	135792		348192	203449

In the articles 24 and 26 of the DFL MOP N° 382/88 is considered another type of sanction to those firms that do not complied with their Development Programs: the cessation of their concessions (in the case that the firms have started the exploitation of the concession, the President of the Republic has the faculty to take these kind of decisions by considering the SISS technical point of view—the case of "Aguacor SA," in region III of Chile, is the unique case registered).

By SISS's decision (or on concessionaries' request) it is possible to modify the Development Plans but good reasons are needed—for example, substantial changes of the projected demand (see article 58 of the DFL MOP N° 382/88). Likewise, those Plans are actualized every 5 years (in each tariff revision).

Time frame of case study	There are several case studies (the first case dates for June of 1996, and the last one, November 1998). The mechanism

(Continued)

---

44. One UTA is equivalent to $356,868, that is, US$512.1 (on December 2003).

Case Study 5: Water and Sewerage in Chile (*Continued*)

Regulatory instrument targeting investment uncertainty	**Extraordinary tariffs revisions in the efficient firm model**
	of extraordinary reviews existed since the regulatory law for the sector was passed in 1988. In February 1998, after the legislation was amended, changes were made to the tariffs for the period in order to compensate for the expenses incurred under the changed situation (tariffs had to be recalculated to reflect these new expenses).
Scope of mechanism	Types of investment covered in the different case studies:
	▓ Quality of raw water: solicits the incorporation to tariffs the augmentation of expenses derived of the need to treat the excess of some not wanted minerals.
	▓ As a consequence of lack of rain for a long period, the company had to lead with lower underground water. This implied to implement new constructions for production and pipelines for allowing to have a higher caudal.
	▓ Higher Opex in order to take into account higher quality standards.
	▓ Changes in the law that regulated the discharges of liquids to the see, which implied the construction of new constructions.
	▓ Of course, this is not an exhaustive list (new circumstances may justify new extraordinary reviews of the efficient firm's planned investments).
Regulatory process	Process is explicitly included in the law. However law does not explicitly specify which type of investments trigger the revision mechanism.
	Appeal. The Expert Commission intervenes if a new study is required.
Symmetry of mechanism	Symmetric because, in principle, the regulation does not set away any investment of the revision mechanism.
Description of mechanism and regulatory treatment of expenses	The article 12A of the Decree with Law Force (DFL) number 70 of 1988 (modified by in 1998) establishes: "Only when exist justify reasons concerning important changes in the assumptions made for the estimation of the tariffs' formulas for the period, the parties [the regulator and the company], exceptionally and by agreement, could modify them before the end of it. The new formulas will last for a new five years period".
Evidence of performance	It is missing the amount of investments recognized by the regulator in each of the case studies.
Opportunity for gaming	Does this mechanism incentive opportunistic behavior?
Primary information sources	DFL 70; D.S. MINECON N° 453 and study cases.

Case Study 6: Electricity Distribution, Chile

Regulatory instrument targeting investment uncertainty	Logging up and down (extraordinary tariff reviews)
Industry concerned	Chilean distribution companies.
Ownership structure	A total of 31 generator, 5 transmission companies and 36 distribution firms participate of the national electric industry. They supply the national aggregate demand which, in 2002, reached the 24.633,3 GWh. The national demand is divided in four territorial areas (SING, SIC, Aysen and Magallanes). Enersis is the holding company for the largest distribution utility, Chilectra, which serves the Santiago metropolitan area (roughly 40% of the total retail market). Chilectra and Chilquinta are the largest of the 17 investor-owned distribution utilities operating in the SIC (Central Interconnected System).[45] Edelnor and two smaller distribution utilities provide distribution service in the SING (the northern system). Generally, small vertically integrated companies under private ownership provide distribution service in the smaller, isolated systems (Edelaysen, Edelmag). There are also 3 small municipal utilities and a few electric cooperatives supplying retail electricity services in remote areas.[46]
Sector background	The electric market in Chile is separated in the activities of generation, transmission and distribution. These activities are developed by firms that are totally controlled by private capitals, while the state only is in charge of regulation, controlling and planning investments in generation and transmission (however this last function is taken only as a recommendation by the parties).
	The institutional structure of the regulatory agencies in the Chilean sector is as follows:
	(1) The principal agency is the **National Commission of Energy** (Comisión Nacional de Energía—CNE). This institution was established by decree in 1978. It undertakes most of the normative and regulatory functions for the energy sector, including proposing policies and strategies

(Continued)

---

45. Four big ownership groups exist in the electricity distribution industry: 1) Chilectra, that is controlled by Enersis; 2) CGE, CONAFE, Emec and Río Maipo, that are controlled the group Real (through CGE); 3) Emel, controlled by PPL; and 4) SAESA FRONTERL and Chilquinta that are controlled by the PSEG Chile holding.

46. Data for the regulated distribution companies:

	1992	1993	1994	1995	1996	1997	1998	1999	2000	2001	2002
RoA	23.2	24.2	26.2	30.1	31.1	31.7	28.1	22.0	24.1	23.4	21.5
RoE	9.9	11.4	12.3	10.3	12.4	11.7	11.9	10.5	9.3	8.5	7.5
D/E (%)	56	44	44	47	47	54	65	79	103	128	130

Source:

Case Study 6:   Electricity Distribution, Chile (*Continued*)

Regulatory instrument targeting investment uncertainty	Logging up and down (extraordinary tariff reviews)
	for the sector, undertaking tariff studies, proposing tariff and self-regulating pricing formulas, establishing regulations, service standards, and operating criteria for sector enterprises; and overseeing the dispatch entities. It also undertakes indicative planning and may recommend state financing of generating (>200 MW) or major transmission projects that are not being pursued by other interests (the agency's 48-month generating projection is used to set node prices and allows CNE to guarantee that enough capacity will be available to meet expected demand). The CNE consists of 7 Ministers (Economy, Finance, Defense, Mining, Planning, Secretary General, and a Chairman that is appointed by the president and has the status of a minister) and an Executive Secretariat headed by a presidential nominee. The member ministries issue decrees implementing CNE recommendations, and ensure policy coordination of the important ministries.
	(2) The **Superintendence of Electricity and Fuels** (SEC), has evolved over decades as an oversight authority under the Ministry of Economy for technical and operating (including safety) compliance of sector entities with sector legal and regulatory requirements and of tariff applications. It may impose data on sector enterprises and sets the New Replacement Value for distribution assets. It may impose penalties or recommend rescission of concession contracts. The President appoints the Superintendent.
	(3) The **Ministry of Economy** authorizes concessions, approves and publishes tariffs proposed by CNE, and generally oversees economic regulation of the sector.
	(4) The **Ministry of Finance** implemented the restructuring and privatization of sector enterprises through the Corporación de Fomento y de la Producción (CORFO). It continues to handle privatization procedures as well as maintains an oversight role in the financial performance of enterprises in which the state has an ownership share.
	(5) **CONAMA** is the environmental protection agency established in 1990 with jurisdiction over environmental issues for the sector.
	(6) The **Anti-Monopoly Commission** is a judicial entity that oversees, investigates, and deliberates issues related to competitions, reviewing anti-competitive charges and cases brought before it.
Form of regulatory regime	The efficient firm approach (see Case Study 5 for explanation).
	Tariffs determinations: the Aggregate Value of Distribution
	According to the Decree with Law Force number 1 of 1982 (DFL 1/82) consumers with load less than 2000 KW are subject

---

Case Study 6: Electricity Distribution, Chile (*Continued*)

Regulatory instrument targeting investment uncertainty	Logging up and down (extraordinary tariff reviews)
	to regulation. The final tariffs charged to these consumers are composed by a price of supply—the node price- and the regulated price of distribution—the aggregate value of distribution (VAD). The first one is recalculated every six month, while the second one, every four years. The VAD (or the tariff of distribution) is obtained using the "efficient firm" logic; that is, a model of an efficient firm is constructed to derive which distribution tariffs should be charged (article 106 DFL 1/82). An important feature is that the efficient firm is constructed for a set of firms grouped in a certain standard area (defined in each tariff revision).[47] The VAD is the median cost of providing the service. So every four years, long run median costs have to be calculated for an efficient firm for each standard area. In each of them, a certain real firm is selected. Considering some fundamental parameters of this firm (geographic zone, density, etc.), the CNE conducts a study to construct an efficient firm adapted to demand. The results obtained from this hypothetical model are applied to all the firms in the area.[48] Firms also have the right to conduct their own studies in order to calculate the values involve in this process.[49] Preliminary distribution tariffs are obtained by weighting the values implied in both costs studies: giving 2/3 to CNE's values and 1/3 to the firms' studies (article 107). Finally, with these preliminary tariffs a "test of returns" is made; according to the DFL 1/82 (article 108). The VNR and the opex declared by each firm at the beginning (see footnote VI) are used to calculate the rate of return of all the firms considering the energy and the power as if they would have been sold by those preliminary tariffs. If that aggregate rate of return is between 6 and 14% the preliminary tariffs are definitive. Otherwise, tariffs are adjusted proportionally to reach the nearest limit.

(Continued)

---

47. The principle variable to determine these areas is the customer density (it is assume that firms with similar density have alike costs). For the last three tariffs revisions: 1992 tariffs determination defined 4 standard areas; 1996:5 and 2000:6. The Tariffs revisions are done for the whole industry (this is different from what happen in telecommunication and water).

48. This was the methodology used in the 2000's tariff revision, but in the earlier tariffs revisions, the mechanism was different because inside each standard area, a geographic zone was selected (from one of the real firms that represents the area) and was for each of these zones that the efficient firm was constructed (afterwards, the results obtained were applied to the geographic zones of the rest of the firms whose density were similar).

49. *The formal process.* The process of tariffs revision starts one year before the tariff revision with the determination of the New Value of Replacement (VNR) and the declaration of opex for every firm. The VNR is the actual cost of acquiring new installations and equipment, that allow to offer (using the newest technology and a minimum cost), an identical service supply by the firms. This information is use later in the tariffs determination process (before fixing the final tariffs) to check if firms' returns are between established parameters. Six month before the new tariffs enter into force, the CNE established the bases of the study for the determination of the costs of the efficient firm and the standard areas. Firms can also do their own costs studies (over that base fixed by the CNE) and have also the opportunity to make observations to the way standard areas were specified (however CNE has the power to set aside these lasts observations).

Case Study 6: Electricity Distribution, Chile (*Continued*)

Regulatory instrument targeting investment uncertainty	Logging up and down (extraordinary tariff reviews)
	For example, if firm i declared VNR_i, opex of c_i, sales by q_i and the preliminary tariff is p_i, then the rate of return for all firms is:
	$$r = \frac{\sum_i p_i q_i - c_i}{\sum_i VNR_i}$$
	If r is between 6 and 14% those preliminary prices are definitive.
	For the last three tariffs revisions: in 1992 the average VAD was of 27338 ($/KW/year). For 1996 the average VAD was 60852 ($/KW/year) and in the year 2000, the average VAD was fixed in 90771 ($/KW/year).
Time frame of case study Scope of mechanism Regulatory process	The DFL 1/82 specify in article 110: "This formulas will have a validity period of 4 years except that […] the economic rate of return before taxes for the distribution companies as whole […] differ in more than 5 points of the actualization rate defined in article 106 [10% annual in real terms]. In these cases the Commission [CNE] must do a new tariff study, except that the concessionaires and the Commission agree unanimously to adjust the original tariffs formula. In the case that a new study must be made, it will last for a new four years period.
	In addition, if before the end of the four year period where the original tariffs are still valid there is a unanimously agreement between the distributions firms and the Commission to make a new tariff study, it could be done and the new tariff's formulas will be valid till the end of that period."
	This mechanism can be used as a not regulated system of logging up and down expenses.
Symmetry of mechanism	In principle the law does not set aside any particular capex or opex of that extraordinary review of tariffs.
Description of mechanism and regulatory treatment of expenses	Still missing to find some study cases where this mechanism was applied.
	Appeal: Experts Panel.
Primary information sources	DFL 1/82; CNE.

Case Study 7: Water and Sewerage Industry in England and Wales

Regulatory instrument targeting investment uncertainty	Ex ante Ex post assessment, logging-up and interim determinations
Industry concerned	England and Wales water and sewerage companies
Ownership structure	There are 10 main water and sanitation companies privatized in 1989 and small(er) water-only companies privately owned since establishment (many established in the nineteenth century). Considerable consolidation among the smaller companies has occurred since privatization with there now being 12 water only companies compared to 23 at the time of privatization.
Sector background	Economic regulation for all water and sewerage and water-only companies has been the responsibility of Ofwat since 1989.
	Investment has been a major issue for the companies—around £50 Billion between 1989 and 2004 much of which was on new quality obligations (as opposed to a value at privatization of about £8 Billion). There are multiple aspects of the regime handling investment—forecast investment is handled through the ex ante/ex post approach described in the case, while unanticipated investment is handled through logging-up. There is also provision for interim determinations.
Form of regulatory regime	The regime was put in place at the time of privatization with 5-year price caps implemented by the industry regulator Ofwat. Originally the regime would allow for price limits to run for ten years (with the possibility of a review being triggered after five years) but all companies agreed to change their licenses following Ofwat's suggestion in 1999 to allow for mandatory five year price reviews.
	Ofwat had triggered a review in 1994 and 1999. There are also provisions for Interim Determinations of Ks (IDOKs) between reviews.
	The system is effectively a hybrid one with metered consumers handled by a price-cap and unmetered consumers handled by a revenue-cap.
	Initial price caps were set by the Government as part of the privatization process.

Regulatory instrument targeting investment uncertainty	Ex ante ex post assessment
Time frame of case study	There are two periods for consideration in this case study:
	▨ 1994–1999 (fixed period approach),
	▨ 2000–2004 (and 2004 to 2009) (rolling period approach)—which is the main focus of the case.
Rationale for using the approach	1994–1999
	The approach taken at the first Periodic Review in 1994 (PR94 consisted of allowing companies to earn a return on the capital value (i.e. the initial value of the assets at privatization plus net new investment (i.e. after allowing for current cost depreciation)—which is described more fully later).

(*Continued*)

Case Study 7: Water and Sewerage Industry in England and Wales (*Continued*)

Regulatory instrument targeting investment uncertainty	Ex ante ex post assessment

The assumption at PR94 was that if there was a review in 1999 the capital base might at that point be taken to reflect the *actual* changes in current cost asset values between 1989 and 1994 while still reflecting the *assumptions* at the 1994 review for the period 1995 to 1999. This working assumption however was the source of discussion immediately post PR94 (discussed below).

There was perhaps little consideration given as to whether the assumptions made in price limits represented a ceiling on expenditure to be allowed in future price limits and the likely assumption by companies would have been that all capex incurred would be remunerated in the future.

The approach taken at the first price review was designed to give some certainty to investors that new capital expenditure would be adequately remunerated (*i.e.* that companies could finance their functions), but also under the system of price caps that higher levels of profitability would result in capital efficiencies being identified and achieved. The 'rolling forward' of the capital value would allow capital efficiencies to be returned to customers in time (albeit ten years after efficiencies were made).

1999–2004

The approach adopted at PR99 (and PR04) was developed over a period of time from PR94 with the main development being that companies were allowed to keep the benefits of any capital efficiencies for a fixed period of five years. How the approach was developed is set out in greater detail below.

There are a number of explanations as to this approach:

▪ That customers would not have to wait too long to see the benefits of capital efficiencies in lower prices (i.e. after 5 years).

▪ That keeping the benefits for a reasonable period of time would provide sufficient stimulus to seek out efficiencies.

▪ To ensure companies had an incentive to seek out efficiencies in capital expenditure regardless of the point in time in the regulatory cycle.

▪ It was relatively simple to operate compared other more elaborate alternatives.

The other major development at PR99 was the explicit use of 'caps'/limits on expenditure *i.e.* expenditure incurred that exceeded the assumed levels (including any logging up) made by Ofwat might be 'dis-allowed' in future price limits. This was also (somewhat controversially) applied at the service level (*i.e.* separate caps for water and sewerage), for the water and sewerage companies, which was introduced late on in the PR99 process. This

Case Study 7: Water and Sewerage Industry in England and Wales (*Continued*)

Regulatory instrument targeting investment uncertainty	Ex ante ex post assessment
	approach also applied retrospectively to expenditure during the 1994–1999 and was highly contested by some companies.
	This mechanism was introduced as a check on companies committing to expenditure that may not be in customer's best interests.
Scope of mechanism	This applies to all capital expenditure (i.e. it includes expenditure related to base service levels, new quality expenditure and expenditure to improve services and balance supply and demand).
Regulatory process	The process of developing the approach to capex was part of an extensive process of consultation the results of whish are set out below. Notwithstanding this Ofwat ultimately decided upon the approach it believes had the appropriate incentive properties.
Symmetry of mechanism	1994–1999
	The question of symmetry did not really arise at PR94. As the approach developed post PR94 it became evident that expenditure might be capped at that level assumed by Ofwat at PR94 (after allowing for any logging up and changes in construction costs). This was applied at the service level although the test at the aggregate level for inclusion was more rigorously applied.
	Some water and sewerage companies and some water only companies incurred greater expenditure on the water service than Ofwat had assumed (including logging up). No companies spent more than was projected for the sewerage service.
	Some companies were allowed to earn a return on the additional capex spent over and above the water service level caps as the expenditure was deemed to be justifiable. A small number of companies, however, had some of the incurred expenditure disallowed from earning a return as it was deemed to have been unnecessary/not of high priority to customers.
	The mechanism between 1994 and 1999 (ex post) was therefore largely (although not entirely) asymmetrical.
	1999–2004
	The approach developed at PR99 was largely again asymmetrical after allowing for any logging up and changes in construction costs with the assumptions on capex being made by Ofwat becoming *de facto* allowances/caps.
Description of mechanism and regulatory treatment of expenses	1994–1999
	At the 1994 Periodic Review the regulatory capital value was determined as a measure of the companies' market valuation around the time of the initial price setting adjusted

(*Continued*)

Case Study 7: Water and Sewerage Industry in England and Wales (*Continued*)

Regulatory instrument targeting investment uncertainty	Ex ante ex post assessment

to take account of the net new capital expenditure allowed for initial price limits. New obligations imposed since 1989 not allowed for at the time and made adjustments for actual changes in national construction prices.

The original capital values placed a direct measure of the value placed by the financial markets on each company's capital by taking the average capitalization of the water and sewerage companies over the first 200 days trading (plus a broadly comparable assessment for water only companies).

At PR94 it was indicated that the approach in terms of capex was to reflect the asset value in regulatory accounts five years before the start of each new price cap in decisions taken at a Periodic Review. For example at the 1999 Review the capital base might at that point be taken to reflect the *actual* changer in current cost asset values between 1989 and 1994 while still reflecting the *assumptions* at the 1994 review for the period 1995 to 1999.

The 'rolling forward' of the capital value would allow capital efficiencies to be returned to customers in time.

In determining the *ex ante* estimates of capital expenditure Ofwat made assumptions about the scope for efficiency savings. A comparative approach was adopted using the so-called cost base which compares typical unit costs for specimen projects ("standard costs"). Companies were placed in efficiency bands with those in the bands of "average" or "less efficient" were required to catch up to the level of the costs of the more efficient companies. In addition all companies were expected to achieve a continuing annual reduction of 1%.

Developing the approach to the regulation of capex

In early 1995 after the review with the suggestions that:

▦ There was a strong case for including capital expenditure of a discretionary nature that had been undertaken to improve services to customers provided this has the support of customers and took account of additional environmental improvements for the environmental regulator.

▦ Outputs not delivered would result in a downward adjustment in the amount of capital expenditure allowed including schemes that were delayed.

▦ If outputs were delivered but at greater cost than allowed for (including any adjustments for changes in legal obligations) then the additional expenditure over and above what was allowed for in price limits would not be allowed (*i.e.* a cap would apply) and the 'inefficiency' would not be rewarded.

In October 1995 Ofwat, however, indicated that "simply adjusting the capital value to reflect actual investment

Case Study 7: Water and Sewerage Industry in England and Wales (*Continued*)

Regulatory instrument targeting investment uncertainty	Ex ante ex post assessment
	with a five year lag is neither necessary nor sufficient. It seems preferable to maintain the link between the capital value and the proper carrying pout of functions." This was in response to companies deferring their capital expenditure (*e.g.* on new quality) and possibly neglecting the state of the assets too (as possibly indicated by problems some companies were experiencing during a drought). In the end a more mechanical approach to capital investment was taken at PR99 partly because of the need to operate a relatively simple mechanism.

1999–2004

At PR99 after consulting on a new approach to the treatment of the RCV Ofwat decided upon the five-year rolling mechanism described above. From 1995–96 onwards for each year the RCV is calculated based on projected bet capital expenditure and actual net capital expenditure where the projected numbers are replaced by actual numbers on a rolling basis. No adjustment is made if the cumulative net capital expenditure exceeds that projected at the previous price review except the excess is attributable to additional expenditure with demonstrable outputs and has customer supports.

This was also applied at the service level (*i.e.* separate caps for water and sewerage), for the water and sewerage companies, which was introduced late on in the PR99 process. This approach also applied retrospectively to expenditure during the 1994–1999 and was highly contested by some companies.

A similar rolling mechanism was also introduced for opex to provide similar incentives to capex but also not to distort the decision between seeking capex or opex efficiencies.

The approach to efficiency was more sophisticated at PR99 than at PR04 with the use again of standard cost for new quality expenditure. For capital maintenance econometric benchmarking and the cost base were applied to determine future levels of maintenance expenditure. |
| Degree of cost pass-through | **1994–1999**

100% of out-turn investment subject to the capping at service level (provided it is below the ex ante estimate including any adjustments for logging up and construction price movements).

Any expenditure in excess would need to be justified in terms of customer benefits. The test would be more rigorously applied at an aggregate level.

See the case on logging up to see how such expenditure is treated. |

(*Continued*)

Case Study 7: Water and Sewerage Industry in England and Wales (*Continued*)

Regulatory instrument targeting investment uncertainty	Ex ante ex post assessment
	1999–2004
	100% of out-turn investment (provided it is below the ex ante estimate including any adjustments for logging up and construction price movements).
	Any expenditure in excess would need to be justified in terms of customer benefits. The test would be more rigorously applied at an aggregate level.
	See the case on logging up to see how such expenditure is treated.
Evidence of performance	Companies have invested substantially since privatization and have largely done this in line with Ofwat's/the Government's initial assumptions.
	There has been evidence of a cyclical nature in investment with companies deferring investment for the immediate year after a price review and then tailing it off again as the next price review occurs. Ofwat have introduced specific mechanism now to try and deal with this ("the early start initiative").
	There is strong anecdotal evidence of companies seeking to find cheaper solutions to capital work issues.
	However there is also anecdotal evidence for at least some companies that the Ofwat assumptions on costs are seen as budgets affecting for example the allocation between opex and capex. Companies may be adopting a lower risk solution to developing the appropriate expenditure plans to deliver a set of outputs rather than fully exploiting potential trade offs.
Opportunity for gaming	Ofwat have tried to link investment of the delivery of outputs and ensure that companies are not able to unduly defer investments—but companies have been able to defer expenditure to some effect.
	There has been the shift of some costs between opex and capex (but not as extreme in the UK electricity distribution sector). In response to this Ofwat have provided regulatory guidance on capex allocation—*e.g.* leakage expenditure to try and remove distortions in the allocation of costs and differences between companies in reporting practices.
Primary information sources	PR94 and aftermath—Ofwat:
	Setting price limits for water and sewerage services, November 1993.
	MD104, *Incentives, benefit sharing and the investment needs of the industry,* 13th April 1995.
	MD106, *Follow on to MD104,* 17th May 1995.
	MD111, *Some key issues for 1995 and 1996,* 9th October 1995
	MD 128, *The regulation of capital expenditure: July return overview,* 27th March 1997.
	Future charges for water and sewerage services, The outcome of the Periodic review, July 1994.

Case Study 7: Water and Sewerage Industry in England and Wales (*Continued*)

Regulatory instrument targeting investment uncertainty	Ex ante ex post assessment
	PR99—Ofwat:
	The proposed framework and approach to the 1999 Periodic Review, A consultation paper, June 1997.
	Setting price limits for water and sewerage services, the framework and business planning process for the 1999 Periodic Review, February, 1998.
	Financial model rule book, a technical paper, October 1998.
	MD143, *Responses to Prospect for Prices,* 15th January 1999.
	MD145, *The framework for setting prices,* 8th March 1999.
	Future water and sewerage charges 2000–05, November 1999.
	Other:
	Dr A. Ballance, The *Privatization of the Water Industry in England & Wales—Success or Failure and Future Directions?,* Stone & Webster Consultants, November 2003.

Regulatory instrument targeting investment uncertainty	Logging up and down
Time frame of case study	Price control period 2000–2005
	The need for an approach to logging-up was first recognized and applied at the 1994 Periodic Review.
Rationale for using the approach	Logging up (and down) is not a formal mechanism like Interim Determinations (see related case-study), but reflects an aspect of Ofwat's approach to price-setting at Periodic Reviews. It is implied by a license requirement to take account at each Periodic Review any changes in circumstances not anticipated at the previous Periodic Review.
	In practice, it deals with smaller changes to the relevant items defined for Interim Determinations, *i.e.* where those are not large enough to trigger materiality.
	Logging up/down applies almost entirely to capital investment. Unanticipated changes in operating expenditures and revenues are automatically dealt with through the re-setting of the starting position for those items at each price review.
Scope of mechanism	Logging up (and down) is applied to the following areas of unanticipated investment:
	A new legal obligation that is enforceable by the quality regulators (Drinking Water Inspectorate or Environment Agency)
	A notified item specified at a previous price review in that it was not or only partially included in price limits.
	A service enhancement that has resulted in a permanent improvement in recorded service level over and above that required as part of the previous review package. Recognition of the change requires evidence of customer support for the improvement.

(*Continued*)

Case Study 7: Water and Sewerage Industry in England and Wales (*Continued*)

Regulatory instrument targeting investment uncertainty	Logging up and down
	Increases in demand for water above those assumed in price limits that have resulted in the need for new investment. The new investment must be shown to be necessary to maintain adequate security of supplies for the foreseeable future.
Regulatory process	*Establishment*

Logging up and down is now an established regulatory process that is intrinsic to Ofwat's price-setting methodology at price reviews. MD179 consulted on Ofwat's proposed approach to logging up and down. This was a response to a perceived need to improve the transparency around the regulatory rules for the treatment of unanticipated expenditures. Ofwat has rejected water company proposals to formalize and codify in the license the approach to logging up. Ofwat argues (in *Setting Price Limits, 2003*) formalizing logging up would encourage intrusive regulation and destroy the benefits of an incentive based approach to price setting.

Implementation

Ofwat's process is summarized as follows:

Companies submit logging up claims in the period 2000–05 as part of the 2004 price review (final claims were submitted in April 2004)

Ofwat's assessment then involves:

Step 1. A "triviality" test. The triviality threshold for a single change is 1% of service turnover in year 3 (at PR04 this means 2002–03) or when aggregated with other small changes is 3% of total service turnover in year 3.

Step 2. Ofwat then assesses if the item is a recognised change not previously provided for in price limits? Recognised changes are normally in the categories note above, but the burden of proof rests with the applicant.

Step 3. Independent verification. Ofwat uses it system of external reporters to confirm that both the solution chosen and the submitted costs are reasonable and properly set down as relevant to the change.

Step 4. Allowance for net additional costs after adjustments reflecting scrutiny by reporters and catch-up factors identified through Ofwat's relative efficiency analyses. No adjustment is made for a company at the efficiency frontier.

Step 5. A second triviality test to establish if the allowed net additional costs associated with the recognised change are above the triviality threshold.

Step 6. Financial adjustments. The reasonable net additional capital costs related to all the recognised items are carried forward into the opening regulatory capital value and so reflected in the return on capital assumptions in future price limits.

Case Study 7: Water and Sewerage Industry in England and Wales (*Continued*)

Regulatory instrument targeting investment uncertainty	Logging up and down
	Appeal
	Companies cannot appeal against Ofwat's logging up and down decisions applied when setting future price limits. The only appeal mechanism currently is to refer Ofwat's price limit determinations to the Competition Commission?
	The Competition Commission will re-consider all price-setting assumptions, including logging up and down.
Symmetry of mechanism	The Ofwat approach is explicitly symmetrical. Items for logging down as well as logging up are considered. Logging down typically applies where changes in obligations, standards or demands not previously recognised in price limits reduce costs or where outputs already financed in price limits are no longer required. Shortfalls—failure to deliver outputs agreed at a previous review—are dealt with in the similar way as logging down, except there is a further adjustment to reflect any "in-period" benefit arising from expenditure not incurred.
Description of mechanism and regulatory treatment of expenses	*Logging up and logging down of unanticipated expenditures.*
	The mechanism makes allowance in prices for the future revenue requirement associated with unanticipated expenditures in the previous review period that passes the Ofwat tests described as steps 1 to 3 above.
	The mechanism only recognises the additional costs from the first day of the next price control period. Logged up or down investment costs are reflected to adjustments in the opening Regulatory Capital Value for the next review period. This means in effect that investors bear any financing costs up to the next review period. Ofwat also make full allowance over the entire asset life for depreciation charges from the first day of the next price control period.
	Shortfalls
	Where logging down occurs due to a failure to deliver agreed outputs, there is an additional adjustment to the allowed level of costs in the next review period. In the case of shortfalls companies do not keep the benefit of anticipated expenditure not incurred. An adjustment equivalent to the present value of the avoided expenditures is made to ensure this.
	Other Issues
	Allowances for logging up and down are also reflected in Ofwat's incentive mechanisms for opex and capex outperformance. Expenditures associated with logging up/down are used to adjust the assumed expenditures profiles at the previous review to ensure the incentive mechanisms are applied to true variances between actual and allowed expenditures.

(*Continued*)

Case Study 7: Water and Sewerage Industry in England and Wales (*Continued*)

Regulatory instrument targeting investment uncertainty	Logging up and down
Degree of cost pass-through	Actual costs are subject to scrutiny by Ofwat's external reporters and application of cost adjustments based on Ofwat's comparative efficiency analysis.
Evidence of performance	Logging up claims were a feature of the 1994 and 1999 Periodic Reviews. The mechanism has largely been used to recognize expenditure associated with new or changed legal obligations related to drinking water and environmental quality standards. Total quality related capital expenditure in the 1995–2000 period was about £8.0 billion, 2002–03 prices). This compares to £10.6 billion, 2002–03 prices initially allowed at the 1994 review.
	MD179 notes that at the 1999 price review about £600m of additional capital investment in the period 1995–2000 was recognized and logged up. If this had been allowed in 1994, Ofwat estimates that prices in 2000–01 would have been 1% higher.
	For the same period about £21m per annum of quality-related operating expenditure was also logged up. Ofwat's estimates this equates to price increases of about 0.5% in 2000–01.
	Company level information on the levels of expenditure claimed for, as opposed to allowed for, is not made publicly available by Ofwat. Companies report annually a commercial-in-confidence analysis of variances in capital expenditures, including any variation attributable to outputs not anticipated at the previous final determination. However, industry level analysis presented in Ofwat's *Financial performance and expenditure of the water companies in England and Wales 2002–2003 report* suggests that about £1.8 billion (2002–03 prices) of total capital expenditure in the period 1995–2000 related to additional outputs not initially anticipated at PR94. This compares to Ofwat's allowance at PR99 for logging up of £0.6 billion.
	During the 2004 price review process, Ofwat has consulted on its approach to logging up regime (in MD179). This reflects concerns that the mechanism is less transparent than formal Interim Determinations and regulated companies have argued for formal codification of the logging up process. Companies have argued the logging up process should aim to put companies in the same financial position as if the obligation had been included in price limits at a Periodic Review or included in an Interim Determination. It is argued that the absence of defined rules in the license contributes to regulatory uncertainty and risk. Implicit in this is the view that the current logging up regime acts as a disincentive to investment.
	Ofwat has not accepted company proposals to codify the logging up rules, but is committed to greater transparency of its process to alleviate concerns about regulatory risk.

Case Study 7: Water and Sewerage Industry in England and Wales (*Continued*)

Regulatory instrument targeting investment uncertainty	Logging up and down
	In the current price control period, for example, Ofwat has committed to recognizing in prices limits from 2005 additional expenditure in the current period on service improvements related to sewer flooding alleviation. Any allowance will be based on demonstrated the investment is justified by scheme-level cost-benefit analysis. (MD183).
Opportunity for gaming	With logging up companies bear some of the cost of additional unanticipated investment until the next price review, whereas the IDOK process allows prices to adjust in the current price control period to reflect unanticipated investment. This could create incentives to maximize unanticipated investment to trigger an interim determination. In practice, there is no evidence that this has occurred given Ofwat requires evidence of external support for the expenditure and has put in place independent expert scrutiny of schemes through its system of reporters.
	The potential for logging down has tended to encourage companies to look for offsetting investment expenditure to be logged up. This allows reporting of actual capex in line with final determination assumptions. To counter this Ofwat has applied strict criteria to items eligible for logging up, with the potential result that economic investments may be disallowed.
	Ofwat's strict approach reflects concerns about informational asymmetries between the regulator and regulated companies. Ofwat believes companies have little incentive to identify items for logging down and every incentive to identify items for logging up.
Primary information sources	Ofwat (2003) *Financial performance and expenditure of the water companies in England and Wales 2002–2003*, August 2003.
	Setting water and sewerage price limits for 2005–10: Framework and approach, March 2003.
	MD183, Flooding from sewers, September 2002.
	MD 179: Logging up and down—dealing with shortfalls in outputs and new requirements between periodic reviews, June 2002.

Regulatory instrument targeting investment uncertainty	Interim determinations
Time frame of case study	Price control period 2000–2005
	Provision for interim reviews written into original the License of Appointment. The provisions were used to trigger 19 Interim Determinations in the first price control period (1990–95), mainly due to RCC(4), see below. Only one Interim Determination was triggered in the 1995–00 period, due to RCC(1) (again see below for description)
	Shipwreck clause (see below) was removed or revised by Ofwat at 1994 Periodic Review by agreement with appointees.

Case Study 7: Water and Sewerage Industry in England and Wales (*Continued*)

Regulatory instrument targeting investment uncertainty	Interim determinations
	Ofwat subsequently in current period has sought to re-instate this ship-wreck clause in all licenses to achieve greater regulatory consistency (MD167). MD168 indicated all but 3 (subsequently 2) companies had agreed to the re-insertion of the ship-wreck clause)
Rationale for using the approach	Interim reviews of price limits between periodic reviews to take account of unanticipated expenditures attributable to changes in a number of prescribed circumstances. Interim Determinations (IDOKs) are not "mini" price reviews, but designed to cater for specific events for which no allowance was/is made at a preceding price review and which have a material impact on the finances of the business.
Scope of mechanism	Condition B of licenses allows for:

14(2): Interim reviews only triggered in the event of defined "Relevant Items"—Relevant Changes of Circumstance" (RCCs) and/or Notified Items.

Currently a maximum of 4 RCCs original licenses at privatisaton has 8, but this was reduced by Ofwat by agreement with companies at the 1994 price review:

▓ RCC(1)—New or changed legal requirement;

▓ RCC(2)—Differences in proceeds from land disposals to that assumed at previous price review;

▓ RCC(3)—Failure to meet some output provided for at previous price review;

▓ RCC(4)—Movements in Construction Price Index relative to general price index (this RCC is only provided for in 4 licenses)

▓ Notified Items—these are defined items which, at the previous periodic review, Ofwat recognises as having not been allowed for (either in part or at all), due typically to uncertainty about the scale of costs. In the current period these are limited to: take up of free optional meter installations, bad debt due to ban on disconnections and costs associated with implementing Government guidance on tariffs for vulnerable groups.

Price limits are reset if RCCs and/or notified items exceed a materiality threshold defined as 10% of turnover in last reported financial year.

▓ 14(3): So called "Shipwreck clause"—allows prices to be reset if the appointed business suffers a substantial adverse effect or enjoys a substantial favourable effect not attributable to management action

Price limits are reset if impacts exceed a materiality threshold of 20% of turnover in last reported financial year.

Both mechanisms are specified in terms of a case-specific present value sum of:

Case Study 7: Water and Sewerage Industry in England and Wales (*Continued*)

Regulatory instrument targeting investment uncertainty	Interim determinations
	▓ Capital expenditure impacts (positive or negative)
	▓ Annual Operating expenditure impacts (positive or negative)
	▓ Annual tariff revenues (positive or negative)
Regulatory process	Formal process is detailed in licenses of the regulated companies—Condition B Clause 14 for Water and Sewerage businesses and Clause 13 for Water only Companies. The actual process in practice is described as follows:
	Ofwat publishes details of its methodology and approach (including interim review financial model) in advance of any applications;
	Formal applications are submitted by 30 September (the mid-point of the financial year), with any revised price limits taking effect from 1 April in the next financial year.
	Ofwat issues a provisional decision on revised price limits based on its assessment of whether:
	The claimed costs arise from any of the defined circumstances;
	Each item must individually satisfy a triviality threshold defined as the present value of an item exceeding 1% of turnover. Items below the 1% threshold are rejected and are not put forward to the materiality test. Ofwat intends to revise this to 1% of turnover by service which is a response to water and sewerage company views that the 1% of total turnover represents too high a threshold.
	The combined present value of all items passing triviality is then assessed against a 10% (of turnover) materiality threshold;
	If the materiality threshold is exceeded, Ofwat issues provisional new price limits for the remainder of the review period;
	Appointed businesses and other stakeholders make representations on the draft decisions by Ofwat
	Ofwat issues it final determinations for the interim review, normally within 2–3 months of the application.
	Revised price limits take effect from 1 April of the following financial year
Symmetry of mechanism	Interim determinations can be initiated both by the company and the regulator. Initially, interim reviews for Notified Items were asymmetrical. Ofwat issued license modifications for Optional metering notified items following Competition Commission re-determination of price limits for Mid Kent Water and Sutton & East Surrey Water in 2000. To date, Ofwat has modified 4 licenses. MD189 proposes the license modification for all appointees.
	MD157 introduced a revised materiality calculation. This was in response to a perceived bias towards capital related expenditures in the calculation. The revised calculation is

---

Case Study 7: Water and Sewerage Industry in England and Wales (*Continued*)

Regulatory instrument targeting investment uncertainty	Interim determinations
	designed to treat capital expenditures symmetrically with operating expenditure and tariff revenue impacts. A 10% capex impact is equated to a 1% annual revenue required impact by calculating the present value of recurring annual impacts as a 15 year annuity.
Description of mechanism and regulatory treatment of expenses	The basic principle of the IDOK mechanism is that the unanticipated expenditure is treated as if the changed circumstances were known at the previous review and prices are adjusted retrospectively to reflect the new costs.

The 2000–05 Materiality Calculation

The materiality calculation is used to determine the magnitude relative to the size of the overall business based on the present value of the cash flows associated with the unanticipated change in circumstances. The same materiality calculation applies to RCCs/Notified Items (labelled by Ofwat in MD189 as "standard IDOKs") and the shipwreck clause, though the thresholds differ.

RD 14/00 sets out the detail of the revised calculation.

Previous to the 1999 price review, the net present value of each element of "Base Cash Flows" associated with each relevant item was calculated over all years up to the first Charging Year to which the next Periodic Review of price limits would apply.

Where the "Base Cash Flows" represent recurring annual costs this calculation can be expressed as the formula:

$$Net\ Present\ Value\,(Base\ Cash\ Flow_{it})$$

$$= \frac{Base\ Cash\ Flow_{it}}{r} \cdot \left(1 - \frac{1}{(1+r)^{T-t}}\right)$$

where T would denote the final Charging Year of the current review period, t denotes the year in which the Base Cash Flow is deemed to be incurred and i ($i = 1, \ldots, n$) denotes the separate costs constituting the Base Cash Flows.

For one-off capital expenditures (such as meter installation) under this calculation rule the net present value is simply defined as the actual expenditure discounted or inflated as appropriate by the discount rate to take account of capital expenditure not timed to occur in the actual year of the IDOK application.

The modified rule calculates the net present value of a "Base Cash Flow" according to the category of cost. The above formulation is retained for costs (net of receipts and savings) that relate to one-off capital expenditure. For categories of recurring cost (net of receipts and savings)—*i.e.*

Case Study 7: Water and Sewerage Industry in England and Wales *(Continued)*

Regulatory instrument targeting investment uncertainty	Interim determinations

revenue loss and operating expenditure—the formula that is prescribed is:

$$Net\ Present\ Value\ (Base\ Cash\ Flow_{it})$$

$$= \frac{Base\ Cash\ Flow_{it}}{r} \cdot \left(1 - \frac{1}{(1+r)^{15}}\right)$$

This implies the net worth of these categories of recurring annual cost is simply calculated as a 15 year annuity, where the value of the "Base Cash Flow" represents the recurring annual sum. For a cash flow equivalent to 1%, the new formula ensures the NPV just exceeds a 10% capitalized value (at a discount rate of 5%).

The aggregate net present value—defined as the "Materiality Amount"—is the sum of the net present values calculated for each "Base Cash Flow". The threshold for an Interim Determination is triggered when this aggregate net present value equals at least 10% of the last known turnover for the Appointed Business as reported under the terms of Condition F. For applications under the ship-wreck clause the threshold is 20%

Changes to the 2000–05 Materiality Calculation

In MD189, Ofwat is proposing a new materiality calculation that would apply from 1 April 2005. The proposal is to revert to the original formulation for all categories of capex and recurring opex and revenue impacts, though for the latter apply a scaling factor (of 2) to enable a 1% annual cost to equate to a 10% capitalized value.

The need for this further revision reflects difficulties with interpreting the PR99 revision. It is clear, however, that Ofwat's own interpretation as applied in recent IDOKs, is not consistent with its own formulation set out in RD 14/00. The formula applied in practice by Ofwat has been:

$$Net\ Present\ Value = \sum_{s=0}^{15} (1+r)^{-t+s} \cdot Base\ Cash\ Flow_{i,t+s}$$

which requires a 15 year projection of the expense, when the rationale for IDOKs is to recognize unanticipated expenses incurred in the current price control period. Under certain scenarios it is also the case that this formulation will overstate the Materiality amount compared to the original formulation, making it easier to trigger to IDOKs than was originally intended. The proposed revision will also have the potential to overstate the materiality amount.

(Continued)

Case Study 7: Water and Sewerage Industry in England and Wales (*Continued*)

Regulatory instrument targeting investment uncertainty	Interim determinations
	Re-setting prices at IDOKs
	Once materiality is accepted, the IDOK process in effect re-sets all of the remaining price limits in the current price control period based on its assessment of the allowable revenue to be required in each of the remaining years. This allows Ofwat to make assumptions about the phasing of the recovery of the unanticipated expenses up until the next price control period. Phasing must ensure that the company is no worse-off in terms net present value terms.
	Under the current rules, the allowed cost of capital for an IDOK varies across the licenses (this implies the discount rate used in the materiality calculation also varies as the same rate is used). At the 1994 review 12 companies agreed to have their allowed cost of capital at IDOKs to be specified as the cost of debt. For the remainder, the specified cost of capital is the weighed average cost of capital. In MD174, Ofwat proposed to restore uniformity, but this has not been pursued. Assuming the cost of debt is below the WaCC as is typical, for companies with the cost of debt, the likely implication is that it is easier to trigger materiality, but allowed recovery of financing costs is based on the cost of debt only.
Degree of cost pass-through	Ofwat challenges and scutinises all cost impacts both for calculation of materiality and re-setting of price limits. Experience in current period suggests this usually means Ofwat reduces company costs, but in some instances higher costs have also been allowed for individual trigger items when assessing materiality
	Ofwat applies its standard methodologies of industry benchmarks and comparative efficiency analysis to determine allowable costs at interim determinations.
Evidence of performance	▓ 12 water companies have made applications for interim determinations in the period 2000–2004 under either the RCC/Notified Items or Shipwreck Clause
	▓ 2 applications have been made under the Shipwreck clause
	▓ Ofwat has rejected 2 applications on the grounds on non-materiality. The rejections take account of counter-claims from the regulator.
	▓ The 10 successful applications have resulted in significant upward revisions to price limits, though typically the cost allowances made by Ofwat are less than that claimed by water companies.
	▓ The 8 successful applications not related to the Shipwreck clause have related primarily to Notified Items (Optional metering and bad debt), RCC1 and RCC4.

Case Study 7: Water and Sewerage Industry in England and Wales *(Continued)*

Regulatory instrument targeting investment uncertainty	Interim determinations
	▦ Allowed investment related costs have mainly been in the specific areas of:
	▦ Meter installations, new requirements on water and effluent quality requirements and relative movements in construction prices
Opportunity for gaming	There is some limited evidence of gaming. The two rejected applications were for the same company (Anglian Water).
	The actual Materiality calculation applied by Ofwat in the current price control period is not consistent with its own stated formulation. The formula it has applied uses projected expenses (beyond the current price control period) and this may afford opportunities to manipulate inputs to the materiality calculation to trigger IDOKs, without affecting the level of expense to be remunerated in revised price limits in the current regulatory period.
	A more important regulatory issue is the present lack of consistency in the IDOK rules for each license. This means that the same materiality thresholds can be exceeded in different companies with different levels of unanticipated expenditures. This implies that the level of protection afforded by the IDOK mechanism is not uniform across the regulated companies.
Primary information sources	In the current review period, Ofwat has issued the open letters:
	MD 189: Proposed license modifications consultation, March 2004.
	MD 186: Interim determinations 2003, May 2003.
	MD 181: Consistency review of companies' license conditions, October 2002.
	MD 178: Interim Determinations 2002, May 2002.
	MD 174: Consistency review of companies' license conditions, December 2001.
	MD 169: Interim Determinations 2001, May 2001.
	MD 168: Modification of conditions of appointment— proposal about condition B, part IV (interim determinations), April 2001.
	MD 167: Modification of conditions of appointment— proposal about condition B, part IV (interim determinations) and other possibilities. Appendix—the 'Shipwreck Clause', January 2001.
	MD 167: Modification of conditions of appointment— proposal about condition B, part IV (interim determinations) and other possibilities, January 2001.
	RD 14/00: Notified item for meter optants, May 2000.
	MD 157: License modification—Condition B, January 2000.

Case Study 8: Electricity Transmission in England and Wales

Regulatory instrument targeting investment uncertainty	Connection charging regime and the error correction mechanism
Industry concerned	Electricity transmission in England and Wales.
Ownership structure	Single private company owning, and responsible for the operation of, the transmission network.
Sector background	National Grid Company (NGC) owns and operates the high voltage electricity transmission system in England and Wales. NGC was created in 1990 during the restructuring of the industry and was originally owned by the twelve regional electricity companies (RECs) created at the same time. In 1995, NGC was floated after a number of the RECs demerged their shareholdings in the company. NGC has two important functions: transmission asset owner (TO) and system operator (SO)—both are regulated by OFGEM.
Form of regulatory regime	NGC has two main types of charge: connection and use of system charges. Connection charges are designed to reflect the costs of connecting particular users (such as a generator) to the existing transmission system. Use of system charges vary by location and reflect the different costs of providing the transmission at different locations. These costs vary depending on the balance of generation and demand at different points on the system.
	NGC's methodology is based on a "shallow connection" approach. Under this approach any transmission system reinforcement costs that result from new connections are recovered through use of system charges and not from new connectees through connection charges. A key element of this methodology is how different connection assets are defined—some assets are classified as infrastructure assets and others as connection assets. The costs of infrastructure assets are recovered from everyone using the transmission system through use of system charges as the infrastructure assets are being used by and benefits everyone that are connected to the transmission system. The costs for connection assets are recovered from the market participant(s) making use of those particular assets.
	NGC's connection charges comprise:
	▪ A depreciation charge over the appropriate depreciation period based on the Gross Asset Value ("GAV") of the relevant assets, net of any capital contribution paid by the customer.
	▪ A return on the un-depreciated value (Net Asset Value, or "NAV") of the relevant assets, taking account of any capital contributions paid by the customer, and
	▪ Charges relating to the ongoing operation and maintenance of the assets (based on annual average costs and expressed as a percentage of the GAV).
	In addition to basic connection charges, users may pay NGC for other specific costs related to their connection. These include one-off charges such as for relocating or

Case Study 8: Electricity Transmission in England and Wales (*Continued*)

Regulatory instrument targeting investment uncertainty	Connection charging regime and the error correction mechanism

diverting existing transmission lines, land charges necessary where NGC purchases land to facilitate a connection, consent costs and rental site costs incurred when NGC owns a site embedded within a distribution network. More specifically, Paragraph 6.6 of the Connection and Use of System Code (CUSC) and Appendix B of NGC's standard Bilateral Connection Agreement define NGC's Connection Charging terms. These connection charges comprise six elements:

- Charges relating to pre-vesting assets (*i.e.* in existence before 31st March 1990).
- Charges relating to post-vesting assets.
- Charges relating to Energy Metering Systems assets.
- Land charges.
- Miscellaneous charges.
- One-off/Transmission charges.

In the majority of cases, these Connection Charges are payable in equal monthly installments. However, some customers make capital contributions to connection charges and some pay accelerated depreciation charges for connection assets.

The decision whether or not to make a capital contribution is up to the customer and is essentially a cash flow issue— if the customer has sufficient cash they may chose to finance some or all of the asset cost up-front so as to avoid finance charges. The asset still counts as part of NGC's capital base and so they will earn a return upon it. Accelerated depreciation usually occurs when the connection asset is expected to have a longer life than the asset to which it is being connected. Apparently this has happened in the context of some gas fired power stations that are expected to have a relatively short lifespan.

Another form of fee levied by NGC is Termination Charges which relate to payments made by a customer choosing to disconnect from the transmission system. Historically there have been three kinds of termination charge:

- Type A terminations relate to connection assets made redundant by the disconnection of a party and reflect the net asset values (NAV) of the appropriate connection assets.
- Type B termination charges are also based on the NAV but are levied on the allocated NAV for any shared assets that are not made redundant. Type B termination charges are used to protect the remaining user's capital charges *i.e.* existing users should not be punished via higher capital charges because another user decides to terminate. Users who have terminated are

(*Continued*)

Case Study 8: Electricity Transmission in England and Wales (*Continued*)

Regulatory instrument targeting investment uncertainty	Connection charging regime and the error correction mechanism
	refunded an appropriate proportion of their termination charge if the asset is subsequently reused (there are specific definitions as to what constitutes reuse) either as a connection or infrastructure asset. Type B terminations may also be refunded if a new user connects at the site, or if a remaining user modifies their connection.

■ Finally, NGC may levy "making good" charges *i.e.* costs associated with securing the terminated site.

The proposed changes to the connection boundary under "Plugs" means that there will be no shared connection assets and therefore Type B termination charges are no longer required. Type A termination charges and making good charges will remain.

In terms of implementation, Termination charges are taken from the Termination Security Deposit that users are required to make at the time of signing their connection agreement.

A further important aspect of the regulatory regime concerning connection assets is that there is competition for providing connection services. More precisely, there are contestable and non-contestable aspects of connection. NGC is the provider of monopoly (*i.e.* non-contestable) aspects of connection and also acts as connector of last resort for contestable aspects of connection.

The majority of connection activities are contestable—the customer can choose to install the connection assets themselves or get a contractor to do it for them. Where the required assets will extend and form an integral part of NGC's transmission system (*e.g.* new overhead lines), they are defined as non-contestable and NGC will perform the work.

NGC's TO functions are regulated by means of periodic review of relevant activities and the setting of a price control. Under this approach, Ofgem sets the allowed revenue of the company. The allowed revenue is based on an assessment of efficient capital and operating expenditure over the period, together with an assessment of efficient financing costs required to fund the business.

NGC's existing TO and SO internal cost controls are intended to last until 31st March 2006. However, Ofgem has proposed extending this until 31st March 2007 in order for it to align with price control review dates for other transmission asset owners in both electricity and gas.

NGC's TO price control is an RPI-X form of revenue restriction. The allowed revenues were related to a set of outputs, expressed in terms of the levels of transmission capacity to be provided on NGC's transmission system.

The revenue restriction includes a revenue adjustment mechanism which comes into play if the quantity of new

Case Study 8: Electricity Transmission in England and Wales (*Continued*)

Regulatory instrument targeting investment uncertainty	Connection charging regime and the error correction mechanism
	generation connections (or level of interconnector capacities) is higher or lower than the levels specified by Ofgem at the time of the price control review and set out in NGC's license. This revenue restriction term is known as the Gt term and it adjusts NGC allowed revenue to reflect the additional (or reduced) financing costs associated with the capital investment.

Regulatory instrument targeting investment uncertainty	Connection charging regime
Time frame of case study	Price control period 2001–06 (to be extended to 2007)
Rationale for using the approach	NGC is required by its transmission license to keep its Connection Charging Methodology and Use of System Charging Methodology (the 'Charging Methodologies') under review at all times. NGC's must bring forward proposals to modify its Charging Methodologies that it considers will better facilitate achievement of the relevant objectives set out under the transmission license. These objectives are: facilitating competition; ensuring charges reflect costs; and ensuring that charges take account of developments in NGC's transmission business. NGC also has license obligations not to discriminate between different classes of customers and not to set charges that restrict or distort competition in generation, transmission, distribution or supply.
	In February 2002, NGC initiated a review of its connection charging methodology. The review focused on the extent to which NGC's connection charges were genuinely shallow. Shallow connection charges may be considered to promote competition in the provision of new connections and to promote competition in the wholesale market by ensuring that all generators can access the transmission network on equivalent commercial terms. NGC developed a model for changing its connection charging methodology called the "Plugs" model. Under this model, connection charges would become shallower as some assets that are currently treated as connection assets would be treated as infrastructure assets. The costs of these assets would be recovered from use of system and not connection charges.
	NGC's proposal was accepted by Ofgem in December 2003. A consequence of the change is that NGC's revenue from connection charges will fall substantially. Under the old license arrangements, NGC's use of system revenues would not rise automatically. As Ofgem set a price control from April 2001 that fixed NGC's allowed revenue, Ofgem has decided to modify NGC's license to ensure that NGC can recover its allowed revenue. As revenues from connection charges will fall, use of system charges and revenues will rise to allow NGC to recover the total revenues allowed under the April 2001 price review.

(*Continued*)

Case Study 8: Electricity Transmission in England and Wales (*Continued*)

Regulatory instrument targeting investment uncertainty	Connection charging regime
Scope of mechanism	Applies to all new and existing parties connecting to NGC's transmission network.
Regulatory process	NGC presents proposal for altering its connection charging methodology to Ofgem for approval. Ofgem then conducts a consultation exercise before delivering its conclusion.
Symmetry of mechanism	Symmetrical—reduction in allowed connection revenues are compensated for by an increase in revenues accruing from use of system charges.
Description of mechanism and regulatory treatment of expenses	The agreed modification to NGC's connection charging methodology has four key elements:

▓ Change to connection boundary: All assets which are shared or could be shared will be charged for via use of system charges rather than connection charges to which a different methodology applies. Sharing of transmission assets would therefore only occur within use of system and not connection. This means that substations (and associated site infrastructure and land), generation only spurs, and shared transformer circuits will be charged for via use of system charges.

▓ Removal of land charges: All connection assets that previously attracted a charge for land will be charged for via use of system charges. Land charges have therefore been removed from the connection charging methodology.

▓ Removal of type B termination charges: Type B termination charges were levied against users that are departing a connection site with shared assets. The change to the connection boundary will ensure that assets which are shared or have the potential to be shared are charged for via use of system charges. Type B termination charges have therefore been removed from the connection charging methodology.

▓ Change to calculation of site specific maintenance charges: Previously, NGC apportioned the total forecast maintenance costs to users based on a three year historic average of costs at the specific sites. For assets that were less than three years old, an assumed fixed maintenance factor of 0.5% of Gross Asset Value was applied. With the modification, NGC will charge users site specific maintenance based on cost pass through of actual maintenance costs incurred in the relevant year. The charge will also include a proportion of maintenance overheads such as costs related to maintenance planning and management activities. The maintenance overheads will be apportioned between connection and use of system assets relative to the Gross Asset Value of these assets. Indicative site specific charges will be based on a flat percentage of the Gross Asset Value (estimated at 0.5% for the year 2004/05). There is then a one-off reconciliation against

Case Study 8: Electricity Transmission in England and Wales (*Continued*)

Regulatory instrument targeting investment uncertainty	Connection charging regime
	actual outturn charges in July of the year following the year the charge relates to.
Degree of cost pass-through	Cost pass through of site specific maintenance costs only.
Evidence of performance	The new charging methodology only came into effect in April 2004, so it is too early to evaluate its performance. However, in accepting the proposals, Ofgem made the following points:

- Under the old connection arrangements, discriminatory charges could potentially arise. This was because a user's connection charge may depend on other users' requirements for shared assets and the particular configuration of the transmission system at the point of connection whereas all users were charged by NGC for wider transmission upgrades. The new methodology will help ensure there are non-discriminatory arrangements for connection to and use of the system helping to ensure that all users face a level playing field.

- The proposed modification will ensure that the costs of all assets that are shareable are charged to all users, as these assets ultimately can benefit all users of the transmission system. Ofgem considers that this will improve the cost reflection in NGC's charges and cost-reflective charges encourage efficient use of the system by giving appropriate signals as to the costs of locating at different points on the transmission system.

- The change will improve the transparency of connection charges as the old methodology could be seen as arbitrary in some cases, as a user's connection charge may be influenced by the actions of other users (especially at shared connection sites). Ofgem considers that the modification removes this potential for arbitrariness in charge setting, enhancing both cost reflection and competition in generation.

- The new methodology will remove risks associated with sharing assets. Previously, the charge of a user at a shared site could change significantly if another user, for example, requires an upgrade to the connection or disconnects and leaves the site. The change will remove the potential for volatility in charges to users as all shareable assets will be charged via use of system charges. Again, this should promote competition.

- Charging for shareable assets via use of system charges will make it easier for users to undertake maintenance on contestable connection assets. Ofgem also considers this may provide more scope for competition in carrying out connection works on the remaining connection assets.

- Where assets are shared, such as at shared connection sites, the roles of responsibility for particular assets may previously have been blurred to the extent that it may

(*Continued*)

Case Study 8: Electricity Transmission in England and Wales (*Continued*)

Regulatory instrument targeting investment uncertainty	Connection charging regime
	impact on the wider transmission system. The new methodology removes any potential for blurred responsibilities, as all shareable assets will become part of infrastructure, and as such will be the responsibility of NGC.
	An important outstanding issue remains in relation to NGC establishing clear principles for addressing repayments to users for legacy issues. Some customers have paid for connection assets in a lump sum rather than over the life of an asset. With the change in charging methodology, some of these assets have become infrastructure assets and customers are entitled to have an appropriate proportion of the lump sum payments refunded. This raises an issue of how such payments from NGC to customers are funded. As NGC is effectively purchasing infrastructure assets the expenditure could be treated as capital expenditure in the normal way with NGC receiving depreciation and financing costs through an adjustment to its price control revenue over the life of the asset. Alternatively, if the payments were treated as revenue, the allowed revenue under the price control could be increased to cover the costs of the refunds as they are made. NGC have indicated that the likely amount of refunds is in the order of £60m.
	Ofgem has indicated that is prefers the former approach, but is awaiting bilateral negotiations between NGC and the affected parties to get fully underway before making a decision.
Opportunity for gaming	Limited—the change in methodology is designed to make connection charging more equitable and to reduce barriers to entry.
Primary information sources	Ofgem (2003), Decision in relation to Connection Charging Methodology Modification–07.
	NGC (2003), Conclusions Report to the Authority. Modification Proposal to the Connection Charging Methodology.
	Ofgem (2003), Potential changes to NGC's transmission license consequential to possible changes to its transmission charging methodology. A consultation document.

Regulatory instrument targeting investment uncertainty	Error correction regime
Time frame of case study	Price control period 2001–06 (to be extended to 2007)
Rationale for using the approach	Uncertainty in the generation market that existed at the time of NGC's 2000 price review meant that future generation connections could, according to NGC, lie anywhere in the range of 5–20 GW. Specifically, this uncertainty arose from the introduction of New Electricity Trading Arrangements (NETA) in 2001 and, more importantly, with respect to the amount of new generation capacity necessary to be constructed in order to meet the government's call for renewable generation to provide 10% of UK electricity by 2010. As a result, OFGEM proposed that it should recognize

Case Study 8: Electricity Transmission in England and Wales *(Continued)*

Regulatory instrument targeting investment uncertainty	Error correction regime
	the uncertainty associated with new generation connections by introducing an ECM.
	NGC's load related expenditure (LRE) is affected by the level of new generation connecting onto the transmission network and the resulting closure of generation. Most of the factors affecting whether and when new generators connect are outside NGC's control. Therefore, any differences between actual and forecast expenditure will not be the result of either efficiency or inefficiency on the part of NGC. In reaction to this situation, Ofgem noted:
	Although Ofgem considers it appropriate for NGC to be exposed to the financial impact of its efficiency performance, exposing NGC to the impact of factors beyond its control could increase business risk and raise NGC's cost of capital.
	The introduction of a logging up mechanism was discussed to account for the possibility of non anticipated LRE, but in the end the Gt term was chosen to reduce the effects of uncertainty on the business and to put in place a transparent mechanism.
Scope of mechanism	Gt term applies only to LRE associated with generation connections and interconnector capacity.
	Non-anticipated load-related expenditure caused by generation connections above or below a central value determined at the 2000 price control review.
Regulatory process	NGC provides evidence to Ofgem that generation connections are above (below) the annual capital expenditure figure and receives an appropriate revenue adjustment.
Symmetry of mechanism	Symmetrical—allowed revenues are increased or reduced by the same amount for above or below realization of connection capacity.
Description of mechanism and regulatory treatment of expenses	Mechanism works as follows: 1. In the course of the price review, a year-by-year estimate of capital expenditure is made. For the current five year price review, a total of 5 GW was forecast over the period. 2. Each year a comparison is made to the forecast level of capital expenditure and for every 1 GW that NGC is either above or below its target, an adjustment of £23 million is made to its asset base. The £23m figure was proposed by NGC to Ofgem during the consultation for the current price control. 3. The revenue impact on NGC comes through its allowed rate of return on its assets plus depreciation. NGC's allowed rate of return is presently 6.25% while depreciation is 2.5% (a forty year asset life is assumed). Consequently, every £23 million adjustment up or down, has a revenue impact of approximately £2.07 million.

(Continued)

Case Study 8: Electricity Transmission in England and Wales (*Continued*)

Regulatory instrument targeting investment uncertainty	Error correction regime
	Signed connection and use of system agreements provide the basis of assessing LRE caused by generation connections.
Degree of cost pass-through	Indirect in the sense that NGC's asset base is automatically adjusted by £23m/GW with subsequent revenue implications.
Evidence of performance	The Gt Term is applied each year. To date, actual and forecast capital expenditure have been relatively close. There have been some small adjustments arising from revisions in connection charging boundaries but the large scale revisions arising from major new renewable generation investment have yet to occur.

The mechanism has been criticized for a number of reasons:

1. Presently there is no equivalent regime in place for Scotland which is where much renewable generation investment will take place. At the very least, therefore, the mechanism would need to be extended to cover the region.

2. The £23 million figure is a very rough estimate of the incurred cost of connecting 1 GW of generation.

3. Ofgem typically dislikes adopting either cost pass through or lump sum (like the Gt term) compensation mechanisms preferring instead to use incentive programmes. The term will therefore likely be replaced by some such approach.

4. The Energy White Paper setting out the renewables generation target was published in 2003 and therefore came into effect after the price control (and associated capacity forecast) was set. The white paper has resulted in multiple renewable generation planning applications to be made and this information can be included in NGC's capacity forecast thereby somewhat mitigating the need for the Gt term.

The scale of renewable generation capacity forecast to be built in the next six years and the desire not to hinder such investment are the principle motivations behind reviewing the approach. Ofgem has launched a consultation process into an appropriate mechanism for funding transmission investment for renewable generation. A preliminary consultation in October 2003 set out three options—taking no action before the next transmission price control reviews (in 2006), re-opening the current price controls or adding an adjustment mechanism to the existing price controls. The first two of these options were rejected as being inappropriate and so Ofgem has decided to develop an adjustment mechanism to supplement the existing price control arrangements. It has set out three options for calculating this adjustment mechanism:

■ Lump sum allowance similar to existing price controls— this could be determined from the forecast level of

Case Study 8. Electricity Transmission in England and Wales (*Continued*)

Regulatory instrument targeting investment uncertainty	Error correction regime
	efficient investment and the associated financing arrangements. Where practicable a set of outputs would be identified (for example increases in network capacity).
	▓ Revenue driver that would provide licensees with predetermined increases in revenue as new investment resulted in an increased demand for network capacity or as additional generation connected to the network. This revenue driver could be similar to that built into NGC's existing price control (Gt term) but there is a difficulty with this simple approach as transmission investment can be lumpy with different schemes having different unit costs.
	▓ Cost pass through, perhaps with a periodic review which would provide Ofgem with an opportunity to decide whether investment had been efficiently incurred.
	Ofgem's initial view is that a cost pass through approach would not be an appropriate way forward. The other two approaches are under investigation with a decision likely by October 2004.
Opportunity for gaming	Ofgem recognizes that careful scrutiny of proposed transmission investment is required in order to prevent unnecessary investment being carried out.
Primary information sources	Ofgem (2000), The Transmission Price Control Review of the National Grid Company from 2001, Final proposals, p.22.
	Ofgem (2004), Extending NGC's transmission asset price control for 2006/07, p. 7.
	Ofgem (2004), Transmission investment for Renewable Generation, second consultation.
	Ofgem (2004), Transmission price controls and BETTA: Update.

Case Study 9: Gas Distribution in Great Britain

Regulatory instrument targeting investment uncertainty	Pay-as-you-go (upfront funding) and additional incentive mechanism of REPEX
Industry concerned	Gas distribution in Great Britain (England, Wales and Scotland)
Ownership structure	The entire gas transmission and distribution system in Great Britain is owned by a single company, TransCo. TransCo was originally a part of British Gas which was privatized in 1986. Following regulatory interventions and detailed compliance rules, British Gas split in the early 1990s into two companies—TransCo and a supply company (British Gas Supply). Subsequently, in 2003, TransCo was acquired by the National Grid Group—the operator of England and Wales' electricity transmission system.
	A process is underway to divest the local distribution zones, LDZs, from TransCo. Sales are expected to be completed later this summer or during the autumn of 2004.
Sector background	Since privatization in 1986, the gas system in Great Britain has been subject to price and quality regulation—initially through a gas sector regulator, OFGAS, and subsequently through the combined energy regulator, OFGEM.
	Around 250,000 km of gas pipeline are operated by TransCo. Of this around 91,000 km are iron pipe within 30 metres of premises. This is believed to constitute a health and safety risk and so in 2001 it was decided by the Health and Safety Executive (HSE), the government body responsible for health and safety issues, that these pipes should be replaced with plastic pipes over a 30 year period. Work by TransCo has shown that the total amount of pipe to be replaced is 98,000 km since new premises may come within 30 metres of the mains. The planned replacement investment was for over 14,000km of iron mains in the period 2002–2007.
	The following table shows the total size of the gross capex for the gas system over the price control period. As can be seen, the replacement capex is almost 50% of the £4,384m total planned capex. OFGEM allowed capex of £3,000m—this lower number reflects the impact of the pay-as-you-go approach as well as customer and third party contributions to investments.
	Total gross capex for the period 2002–2007:
NTS TO £804m Metering £532m LDZ £996m	
	Replacement £2,072m
Form of regulatory regime	A 5-year incentive based (RPI − X) regime is implemented by the industry regulator Ofgem on the LDZs. The regime is basically a revenue-cap with 35% of the allowed revenue driven by the quantity of gas delivered and 65% fixed.
Time frame of case study	Price control period 2002–07—the fourth price control period.

Case Study 9: Gas Distribution in Great Britain (*Continued*)

Regulatory instrument targeting investment uncertainty	Pay-as-you-go (upfront funding) and additional incentive mechanism of REPEX
Rationale for using the approach	There are two elements of the approach being investigated here:
	1. the approach adopted to handle uncertainty about actual costs; and
	2. the allocation of investment costs between opex and capex.
	Significant health and safety related replacement investment was mandated by a decision of the HSE in 2001. As such, OFGEM needed to make a determination as to how that capex would be funded (except for the small amount which was rechargeable—about £95m of the £2,072m replacement capex).
	It was decided that the capex should be split between a pay-as-you-go approach (direct charge to opex) and a normal inclusion in the RAB approach with the split being based on:
	▓ a view as to the benefits that accrue to existing consumers (pay-as-you-go) and those that accrue to future consumers (inclusion in the RAB); and
	▓ the practical implications for price movements and whether changes would be sustainable—for example, treating all the capex as normal capex and including it in the RAB would have allowed significant price decreases in the short-term but the sustainability of the low prices was questioned.
	Given these considerations a simple 50:50 split was decided for the whole replacement capex.
	The second element was then considered—while a clear program for replacement was being developed it was not possible to forecast with total accuracy the cost of that program (which would depend on the diameter of pipe being replaced etc). Further, there were concerns that the company had not undertaken all the investment expected under the previous price control and consequently a mechanism to protect against gaming as well as uncertainty was needed.
Type of investment costs covered	Iron pipe mains replacement program mandated by the HSE.
Scope of mechanism	Each of the mechanisms relates to different amounts of capex:
	1. the allocation between pay-as-you-go and standard capex inclusion in the RAB applies to all replacement investment that would normally be funded by the company (*i.e.* not rechargeable to a third party). This is £1,977m over the five year period; and
	2. the incentive mechanism applies only to the pure mains replacements which is £1,509m over the five year period.

(*Continued*)

Case Study 9: Gas Distribution in Great Britain (*Continued*)

Regulatory instrument targeting investment uncertainty	Pay-as-you-go (upfront funding) and additional incentive mechanism of REPEX
	The difference between the two is primarily service works (£427m)—it is standard to replace the service pipes at the same time as the mains.
Regulatory process	Items included in price control final determination 2001:
	▓ the split between opex and capex; and
	▓ the supplementary mains incentive was included in the price formula as a new term: R_t.
Symmetry of mechanism	The supplementary incentive scheme applies to both over and underspend, but in different proportions (so not perfectly symmetrical). This is described in more detail below.
Description of mechanism and regulatory treatment of expenses	As noted above, the pay-as-you-go:capex split was determined at 50:50 and applied accordingly.
	For the supplementary incentive scheme the system is complex.
	There is a cap on the total replacement investment for the five year period set at £1,509m. However, in any year the actual spend can deviate. The deviation can take two forms:
	▓ a switch from replacing one diameter type pipe to another diameter pipe (six categories of pipe diameter have been identified); and
	▓ a divergence in the amount of pipe replaced—for each category of pipe there is a base line estimate of kms to be replaced.
	A table of unit costs for each category of pipe and each year was incorporated into the final determination (table 4.25). Using the actual amount of pipe replaced in each year it is possible to calculate out-turn total costs (O). This can then be compared to the price control projection (P) to determine exactly what level of costs will be allowed (A) and consequently what adjustment is needed. The mechanism works accordingly:
	if $O \leq P$, then $A = O + 0.33(P - O)$; and
	if $O > P$, then $A = P + 0.5(O - P)$.
	So, a third of any underspend gets kept by the company (with the remaining two thirds returned to consumers) and a half of any overspend has to be met by the company. This means the incentive is on the firm to minimize costs and underspend, although the cap may create gaming opportunities.
	It would appear that the whole of the correction for incentives is made through opex—so although half of the replacement capex is being included into the RAB, any benefit is one-off and taken through higher revenue. However, the operator would still seem to be earning the standard

---

Case Study 9: Gas Distribution in Great Britain (*Continued*)

Regulatory instrument targeting investment uncertainty	Pay-as-you-go (upfront funding) and additional incentive mechanism of REPEX
	ex-ante ex-post efficiency benefits of underspend (the figure included in the RAB is only adjusted at the end of the price control period). This would suggest that there are two incentives for efficient delivery of replacement capex:
	▓ the standard ex-ante ex-post incentive (but limited to 50% because half the capex is expensed through the pay-as-you-go approach); and
	▓ the supplementary incentive.
Degree of cost pass-through	There is, in a sense, a degree of cost pass-through, at least relating to volume (kms replaced) if not cost.
Evidence of performance	None is yet available. The system is being adjusted to take account of the LDZ sale.
Opportunity for gaming	As mentioned above, the divergence between the overspend and underspend proportions allocated to the company could create gaming opportunities for the company. These will be limited because of the cap on total replacement capex—but it would not be impossible to foresee a situation where underspend is concentrated in the early years and overspend at the end of the price control period.
Primary information sources	*Review of TransCo's Price Control from 2002: Final Proposals,* OFGEM, 2001.
	The Health and Safety Executive's Enforcement Policy for the Replacement of Iron Gas Mains, HSE, 2001.
	Separation of TransCo's distribution price controls—Draft proposals, Annex 3: Replacement Expenditure, OFGEM, 2003.

Case Study 10: Electricity Transmission and Generation in India

Regulatory instrument targeting investment uncertainty	Accelerated depreciation
Industry concerned	Electricity—Transmission and Generation (Thermal)
Ownership structure	Prior to 1991, the entire power sector was under Government ownership (except for integrated private utilities serving certain cities and townships). At the federal level, generation utilities owned by Central Government exist whereas at the State level, the State Government owned vertically integrated State Electricity Boards (SEBs) or generation companies exist.
Sector background	In 1991, with the objective of bringing in additional resources for the generation capacity addition requirement, Government of India allowed private investment in generation through IPPs.
	During the 1990's, various State Governments have embarked on restructuring and reform of their power sectors, at different paces, and under their own Reform Acts. In 1998, the Central Electricity Regulatory Commission (CERC) was set up, with some rationalization of the regulatory functions. In 2003, a comprehensive legislation, Electricity Act 2003, was enacted, replacing all earlier legislations.
	Prior to formation of regulatory commissions, the norms for determination of generation tariffs were determined by the Central Electricity Authority, under the Government of India (see details in Form of Regulatory Regime). To incentivise the private and public investment in generation, Government of India in 1992, changed the depreciation rates to provide a higher (accelerated) rate of depreciation, thus de-linking the life of the asset from the rate of depreciation. Rate of depreciation was revised from average 3.6% on Straight Line Method (SLM) basis for economic life of the thermal generation projects to 5.4% in 1990 and 7.5% in 1992. These depreciation rates provided for recovery of capital costs over a duration lesser than the actual life of the asset and were also much higher than the depreciation rates prevailing in most of the other countries (as mentioned by CERC in its subsequent review).
Form of regulatory regime	Prior to the formation of regulatory commissions, the regulatory functions were shared between the SEB, the State Govt and the Central Electricity Authority (CEA, a technical department under the Ministry of Power, Government of India). There was a cost plus (Rate of Return) regime for generation with the generators getting an assured return on their equity. The financial package and project cost were approved by the Central Electricity Authority and the generation tariffs were computed based on the norms laid down by the CEA through Government notifications.
	In the interim (1998–2003), the CEA retained the function of project cost and financial package approval (a Techno-Economic Clearance), while the function of determination of tariff norms was transferred to the CERC.

Case Study 10: Electricity Transmission and Generation in India (*Continued*)

Regulatory instrument targeting investment uncertainty	Accelerated depreciation
	Post Electricity Act 2003, all aspects of tariff determination are with the CERC in case of generators selling to multiple states (and the respective state commissions for intra state sales).
Time frame of case study	1990 to 2001
Rationale for using the approach	The IPPs were typically being developed under a Special Purpose Vehicle (SPV) structure, with the revenue from the sale of electricity under the PPA being the only source of cash flows.
	The SPVs are highly leveraged, implying large principle repayments.
	Also, debt, with tenure to match the life of the asset/contract, was not available.
	If the depreciation rate reflected the life of the asset, the depreciation component of tariff would be lower than the debt repayment requirements in the initial years. The accelerated depreciation rate enabled earlier cash flows, thus enabling the SPV to meet the debt repayments.
	In certain cases, the higher depreciation rate may still not be adequate to meet the debt repayments (for example, hydel projects have large costs and longer life of the asset). In such cases, the generator is permitted to claim Advance Against Depreciation (AAD) in the tariff to make up for the difference, thereby further advancing the depreciation.
	Thus, the mechanism is intended to achieve a direct link between the cash inflows and cash outflows of the SPV, and is de-linked from the economic or accounting concepts of depreciation.
Scope of mechanism	All depreciable assets, with the depreciation being limited to 90% of the total value. The remaining 10% is the residual value.
Regulatory process	The capital expenditure for determining tariff was based on the financial package set out in the techno-economic clearance of the Central Electricity Authority (CEA). Where the actual expenditure exceeded the approved project cost, the excess expenditure as allowed by the CEA was considered for the purpose of fixation of tariff; Provided that such excess expenditure was not attributable to the generating company. The total capital expenditure after the prudence checks and negotiations then became eligible for depreciation at the rates notified by the Government as per the provisions of the Electricity Supply Act, 1948.
Symmetry of mechanism	Symmetrical since it applies to all capex.
Description of mechanism and regulatory treatment of expenses	As described above.
Degree of cost pass-through	The capital expenditure pass through was based on the financial package set out in the techno-economic clearance of the CEA and any excess expenditure was passed through

(*Continued*)

Case Study 10: Electricity Transmission and Generation in India *(Continued)*

Regulatory instrument targeting investment uncertainty	Advance provisional tariff
	based on the CEA's prudence check. The government specified depreciation norms applied on the capitalized expenses were used for computing the actual depreciation for pass through in the generation tariffs.
Evidence of performance	
Opportunity for gaming	Though there is no general possibility of gaming that can be associated with the concept of accelerated depreciation, there are two potentially adverse outcomes.
	▪ Accelerated depreciation has the impact of increasing tariffs in the early years. This (among other factors) makes the IPP tariffs appear abnormally high at the time of commissioning (though the discussions/decisions are based on the "levelised" tariff over the term of the contract).
	▪ The investor may have reduced incentive to maintain/operate the assets in the later years of the project, since the investment is recovered though the asset still has economic life. This is partly addressed by allowing depreciation only up to 90% of the asset value. The investor continues to earn a return on the 10% for the rest of the term. (A second possible explanation for limiting the depreciation to 90% is that the residual value of the plant (say sale of scrap) is not factored into the tariff.)
	In 2001, the CERC in its terms and conditions of tariffs for generation companies readjusted the depreciation rates downwards, and brought them in the range of 3–4%, which are related to the physical life of an asset. The concept of Advance Against Depreciation remains.
Primary information sources	CERC Order on "Determination of terms and conditions of tariff," 2004.
	CERC (Terms and Conditions of Tariff) Regulations, 2004.

Regulatory instrument targeting investment uncertainty	Advance provisional tariff
Industry concerned	Electricity—Transmission[50]
Ownership structure	Interstate transmission is undertaken by Central Government owned monopoly utility Power Grid Corporation of India Limited (PGCIL) also notified as the Central Transmission Utility (CTU).

---

50. The mechanism applies to generation projects also, though largely for the Government owned generation companies (in case of private investors, the tariff is set in the PPA signed prior to commencement of construction, and the conditions and mechanisms for variations in the tariffs are also set in the PPA). In this case study, the mechanism is discussed in the context of transmission (where it may have higher relevance given the greater degree of potential variability in the project cost), without any loss of generality.

Case Study 10: Electricity Transmission and Generation in India (*Continued*)

Regulatory instrument targeting investment uncertainty	Advance provisional tariff
	Though private investment in transmission is allowed, so far only one transmission project is envisaged under the public private partnership between PGCIL and a leading private power utility, for evacuation of power from a generation plan in Bhutan (at Tala).
Sector background	Prior to 1998, the transmission tariffs were regulated by the Central Electricity Authority (a technical department under the Ministry of Power, Government of India). The concept of Provisional Tariff existed under the CEA regime. Since 1998, inter state transmission is regulated by Central Electricity Regulatory Commission (CERC). CERC first issued an order on the terms and conditions of tariffs in 2001 for a three year period ending March 2004. Subsequently, in April 2004, CERC issued the Regulations on Terms and Conditions of Tariff for a five year period ending 2009. These terms and conditions have laid out procedure and principles involved for approval of the transmission tariffs—both the provisional and final tariffs.
Form of regulatory regime	Cost plus tariffs, with the project cost requiring approval of the regulator.
Time frame of case study	1998 to 2004.
Rationale for using the approach	The completed project cost of a transmission project can be significantly different from the initially expected project cost (due to various uncertainties like unanticipated variations in soil conditions, routing, compensation for right of way, larger completion time resulting in higher Interest During Construction, etc).
	The regulator approves the completed project cost based on the audited accounts submitted by the transmission company, and based on the prudency tests applied by the regulator. This process may be completed well after the commissioning of the project.
	Consequently the Provisional Tariff set by the regulator, based on the transmission company's expectation of the completed project cost, allows for the completed asset to be put into commercial use, even while the rest of the regulatory process of finalizing the project cost and tariff is underway. There is no set rule for what proportion of the costs will be allowed—initially figures around 85% were allowed but more recently figures over 90% have been allowed.
Scope of mechanism	All Capex.
Regulatory process	In case of a transmission system declared under commercial operation on or after 1.4.2004, an application for fixation of tariff is made in two stages:
	1. The transmission licensee may make an application as per Appendix I to the "Terms and conditions of tariff" regulations, for determination of *Provisional Tariff in advance* of the anticipated date of completion of the

(*Continued*)

Case Study 10: Electricity Transmission and Generation in India (*Continued*)

Regulatory instrument targeting investment uncertainty	Advance provisional tariff
	project based on the capital expenditure actually incurred up to the date of making of the application or a date prior to making of the application, duly audited and certified by the statutory auditors, and the provisional tariff shall be charged from the date of commercial operation of the respective unit of the generating station or the line or sub-station of the transmission system;
	2. A generating company or the transmission licensee shall make a fresh application as per Appendix I to the "Terms and conditions of tariff" regulations, for determination of final tariff based on actual capital expenditure incurred up to the date of commercial operation of the generating station or the transmission system, duly audited and certified by the statutory auditors.
Symmetry of mechanism	Symmetrical since it applies to all capex.
Description of mechanism and regulatory treatment of expenses	In cost-based tariff regulations, subject to prudence check by the Commission, the actual expenditure incurred on completion of the project forms the basis for determination of Final Tariff. However, where the implementation agreement or the transmission service agreement entered into between the transmission licensee and the long-term transmission customers provides a ceiling of actual expenditure, the capital expenditure shall not exceed such ceiling for determination of tariff. The scrutiny of the project cost estimates by the Commission is limited to the reasonableness of the capital cost, financing plan, interest during construction, use of efficient technology and such other matters for determination of tariff.
	CERC has noted that the examination of capital cost can be done by it or, if required, the assistance of consultants and any other agency could be obtained at that stage.
	Further, for examining the capital costs, the equipment cost details of the project, the financing package proposed to be used in execution of the project, schedule of construction, and the date of commercial operation of the individual lines/sub-station and the date of commercial operation of the entire scheme in case of transmission system, have to be furnished by the licensee along with the sources and uses of funds. Necessary calculations for interest during construction, financing charges and foreign exchange rate variation during the construction period shall also be furnished, wherever applicable in the formats prescribed by the CERC. Wherever formats are not prescribed, the details are required to be furnished by the licensees clearly bringing out information called for by the CERC.
	To further reduce the investment uncertainty, additional capitalization of the following capital expenditure within the original scope of work actually incurred after the date of commercial operation and up to the cut off date (currently

Case Study 10: Electricity Transmission and Generation in India (*Continued*)

Regulatory instrument targeting investment uncertainty	Advance provisional tariff
	one year from the date of commercial operation) may be admitted by the Commission, subject to prudence check:
	1. Deferred liabilities;
	2. Works deferred for execution;
	3. Procurement of initial capital spares in the original scope of works subject to the ceiling norm specified in regulation;
	4. Liabilities to meet award of arbitration or compliance of the order or decree of a court; and
	5. On account of change in law.
	Provided that original scope of work along with estimates of expenditure shall be submitted along with the application for provisional tariff.
	Provided further that a list of the deferred liabilities and works deferred for execution shall be submitted along with the application for final tariff after the date of commercial operation of the transmission system.
	Any expenditure on minor items/assets brought after the cut off date like tools and tackles, personal computers, furniture, air-conditioners, voltage stabilizers, refrigerators, coolers, fans, T.V., washing machine, heat-convectors, mattresses, carpets, etc shall not be considered for additional capitalization for determination of tariff with effect from 1.4.2004.
	Further, the admissibility of the expenditure after the date of commercial operation is governed by the following:
	1. Any expenditure admitted on account of committed liabilities within the original scope of work and the expenditure deferred on techno-economic grounds but falling within the original scope of work shall be serviced in the normative debt-equity ratio specified in the regulation.
	2. Any expenditure on replacement of old assets shall be considered after writing off the entire value of the original assets from the original capital cost.
	3. Any expenditure admitted by the Commission for determination of tariff on account of new works not in the original scope of work shall be serviced in the normative debt-equity ratio specified in regulation.
	4. Any expenditure admitted by the Commission for determination of tariff on renovation and modernization and life extension shall be serviced on normative debt equity ratio specified in regulation after writing off the original amount of the replaced assets from the original capital cost.
Degree of cost pass-through	Prior to the Electricity Act 2003, the capital expenditure pass through was based on the financial package set out in the techno-economic clearance of the Central Electricity Authority (CEA) and any excess expenditure was passed through

(*Continued*)

Case Study 10: Electricity Transmission and Generation in India (*Continued*)

Regulatory instrument targeting investment uncertainty	Advance provisional tariff
	based on the CEA's/ Regulator's prudence check. The capital cost of new projects established after enactment of the Electricity Act, 2003, which does not stipulate techno-economic clearance/concurrence of the CEA for most types of projects (except hydel), the Commission examines the capital cost in all cases of cost-based tariff regulations.
Evidence of performance	In Interlocutory Application (IA) of PGCIL vs Bihar State Electricity Board and others, regarding the approval of tariff for 315 MVA, 400 kV, 3rd ICT at Biharsharif along with associated bays under Bihar Grid Strengthening Scheme in Eastern Region from 1.10.2003 to 31.3.2004, PGCIL stated that an expenditure of Rs 930.41 lakh was incurred up to 30.6.2003 and expenditure of Rs 331 lakh was anticipated beyond 1.7.2003, till the expected date of commercial operation, *i.e.* 1.1.2004. This total revised estimate of Rs 1261.41 lakh as project cost was higher than the approved cost of Rs 1119.87 lakh. In this case, CERC (on 10.12.2003) ordered that *provisional tariff* allowed is 85% of the tariff corresponding to expenditure of Rs930.41 lakh.
	CERC also directed PGCIL to file the revised petition based on up-to-date audited figures on the date of commercial operation by 30.4.2004 on affidavit along with the revised details along with the details of the loans, in the prescribed proformae, with an advance copy to the respondents (BSEB and others). Thereupon, after hearing, CERC will pass the order on final tariffs for the project.
Opportunity for gaming	Though there is no general possibility of gaming, there is a possibility of overinvestment, since there is no direct incentive for efficiency in project cost. This is addressed through the prudency checks of the regulator, and the dependence on audited statements to determine the actual expenditure.
	It is possible that initial costs will be overstated since there is an expectation of less than 100% allowance and consequently the company would want to minimize the potential initial shortfall that can prove difficult to recoup once the final tariff is approved.
Primary information sources	CERC Order on "Determination of terms and conditions of tariff," 2004.
	CERC (Terms and Conditions of Tariff) Regulations, 2004.
	CERC Order in the matter of—"Approval of tariff for 315 MVA, 400 kV, 3rd ICT at Biharsharif alongwith associated bays under Bihar Grid Strengthening Scheme in Eastern Region from 1.10.2003 to 31.3.2004," 2003.
	CERC Combined Order in the matter of— "Operational norms for thermal generation, Financial norms for rate of depreciation, Financial norms for cost of capital, Surcharge on hydro generation, O&M cost norms for hydro power stations, O&M cost norms for inter-State transmission, O&M cost norms for thermal stations," 2000.

Case Study 11: Manila (Philippines) Water and Sewerage

Regulatory instrument targeting investment uncertainty	Ex-ante ex-post, logging-up and interim determinations
Industry concerned	Manila's Metropolitan Waterworks and Sewerage System (MWSS) which was privatized in 1997.
Ownership structure	As agents of MWSS, the two concessionaires are responsible for the provision of water supply and sewerage services. In 1997, International Operators (Northwest Water for East Zone and Lyonnaise des Eaux for West Zone) were required to have each at least 20% stake in the operating company. Local sponsors are leading conglomerates: Ayala Corporation (East Zone) and Benpres Holdings (West Zone).
Sector background	Decades of underinvestment and low tariffs resulted in deterioration of service, increase in non-revenue water and poor profitability. The MWSS privatization aims to improve service, increase investment, increase operating efficiency and eliminate direct government subsidy/investment. The Asian Financial Crisis in 1997 however, prevented the concessionaires from tapping the debt market for funds to finance their original investment plans. The performance of the two concessionaires has diverged with Manila Water, the East Zone operator, showing marked improvement in service expansion, operating efficiency, financing and profitability. On the other hand, Maynilad Water, the West Zone operator, has decided to terminate the contract. The company is mired in legal wrangle with the MWSS, asset owner.
	Given this background investment in the current price control period, 2003–2007, is expected to be $60–$80m per annum for the East Zone operator.
Form of regulatory regime	Hybrid price cap with rate rebasing every 5 years. Interim price determinations (so-called Extra-ordinary Price Adjustments—EPA) possible in-between rebasing periods however grounds are defined/limited in the contract. Annual inflation adjustment is guaranteed. As a result of the recent amendment of the contract, a Foreign Currency Differential Adjustment was integrated in the tariff structure to enable the concessionaires to sufficiently cover higher foreign debt service resulting from material changes in the exchange rates.
	Manila Water and the regulator agreed to adopt a Key Performance Indicators and Business Efficiency Measures (KPI/BEM) System for the rebasing period 2003–2007. Any major deviations (over or under) from agreed indicators get "logged up/down" and rewarded or penalized in the determination of Opening Cash Position of next rebasing period (2008–2013).
Time frame of case study	▓ First rate rebasing period: 1997–2002 ▓ Second rebasing period: 2003–2007. Logging up/down adopted during this period.
Rationale for using the approach	The logging up/down process enables the concessionaires and/or regulator to recognize major investments or

(*Continued*)

Case Study 11: Manila (Philippines) Water and Sewerage (*Continued*)

Regulatory instrument targeting investment uncertainty	Ex-ante ex-post, logging-up and interim determinations
	expenditures which were not captured in the agreed business plan for the next five years and which fall outside the EPA system. It is also expected to improve transparency in the system.
Scope of mechanism	EPA mechanism: Changes in operating environment which are clearly identified under the Grounds for EPA and will result in more than 1% change in tariff.
	Mutual agreement of regulator and operator: Major programs or projects will be pursued by operator on condition that "prudent and efficient" expenditures will be allowed and automatically included as part of the Opening Cash Position in the next rebasing period.
Regulatory process	*Establishment.*
	Process of logging up/down (outside EPA mechanism) is through mutual consultation and negotiation between regulator and operator and footnoted under the KPI/BEM system.
	Implementation
	▪ Unanticipated OPEX/CAPEX are included as part of the Opening Cash Position in year 1 of new rebasing period.
	▪ No retro-active adjustment.
	▪ Prudency/efficiency review of proposed and actual figures.
	▪ An appeals mechanism in place to address disputes.
Symmetry of mechanism	Symmetrical
Description of mechanism and regulatory treatment of expenses	Non-anticipated CAPEX and OPEX are treated as if happening on the first day of the next price control period and consequently the company is not compensated for the additional spending during the period it was incurred. Shareholders have to bear the entire additional costs for up to 5 years.
	Depreciation period of major fixed assets is normally over the remaining life of the concession. If the regulator chooses to not fully depreciate an asset over the concession life, possible especially towards the end of the period, then the expiration payment increases accordingly. This clearly poses a risk for the operator if there are concerns about the Government's ability to make the expiration payment.
Degree of cost pass-through	Expenditure is not passed-through unchallenged. Actual expenditure is subject to regulatory scrutiny and challenge.
Evidence of performance	Problems encountered by the companies owing to the East Asian Crisis makes any assessment of the first control period difficult.
	Amount of logged up/down non-anticipated expenditures is still minimal. Please note that new business plan and the KPI/BEM were only implemented in 2003.

Case Study 11: Manila (Philippines) Water and Sewerage (*Continued*)

Regulatory instrument targeting investment uncertainty	Ex-ante ex-post, logging-up and interim determinations
Opportunity for gaming	There is incentive for operator to defer un-anticipated expenditures to next rate rebasing, so as not to burden the shareholders of additional equity or debt financing.
	Regulator may agree to defer "necessary but unanticipated expenditures" due to socio-political sensitivity of tariff adjustment.
	KPI/BEM system is still being "tested" by the parties and may require fine tuning in subsequent period.
Primary information sources	▦ Approved business plan for current rebasing period
	▦ Official proposal from operator
	▦ Official proposal from regulator and/or asset owner (MWSS)
	▦ Directive from other regulatory bodies (*e.g.*, Department of Health, Department of Environment and Natural Resources)

Case Study 12: Electricity Transmission in Peru

Regulatory instrument targeting investment uncertainty	Three different regimes coexist: the mechanism of the Law of Electric Concessions (LCE); the system of the BOOT contracts (Build, Operate, Own and Transfer) and the special regimen of concession of ETECEN and ETESUR
Industry concerned	Peruvian electricity transmission industry (specifically we will concentrate on the Principal Transmission System[51]).
Ownership structure	Actually, inside the SEIN (the national interconnected electric system)—that joins 20 departments and more than 90% of the demand of energy of the country—there are three private firms with principal lines: Red Eléctrica del Perú (ISA) (which emerged as a result of the privatization of ETECEN and ETESUR[52] on September of 2002), Transmantaro (Hydro Québec) y Redesur (Red Eléctrica de España). Also, three generators own principal lines: Enersur (Tractebel), Aguaytía through Eteselva (Maple Gas) and Egemsa (Empresa Generadora de Macchu Pichu which is state owned.)
Sector background	The sector is regulated. The principal regulator is the Gerencia Adjunta de Regulación Tarifaria del Organismo Supervisor de la Inversion (GART-OSINERG). It is responsible of fixing tariff in the entire electricity sector (every four years distribution tariffs and every year transmission tariffs). The COES (Comité de Operación Económica del Sistema) has the task of planning the operation of the interconnected system fixing the node price for generation, controls the operation programs, coordinates the maintenance of the grid, calculates the short run marginal costs, calculates capacity and firm energy and guarantees to its members the purchase and sale of energy at short run marginal cost. The Ministry of Energy and Mines (MEM) elaborates the expansion planning of the transmission. These plans are not binding for the industry although it establishes the government's position of which projects are considered desirable.
	In conclusion, all these organizations have certain discretion over the planning of the transmission expansion.
	The public firms invested US$351 millions in the period 1990–2003. On the other hand, the private firms invested US$364 million in the same period.

---

51. In the Peruvian transmission system, lines are classified in Primary and Secondary lines (secondary lines are grouped in generation lines and demand lines—depending on who is using them). GART-OSINERG is responsible for doing this classification every four years (or when a new generator is incorporated to the system). The criteria to establish the difference between primary and secondary lines is conceived in article 132 of the Supreme Decree N 009-93-EM: "Reglamento de la Ley de Concesiones Eléctricas": the primary ones are those of very high or high tension (over 100 KV and between 30 KV and 100 KV). The law has two further requirements: the line has to allow bidirectional flows of energy and that the system does not have to allow the identification of individual responsible of the use of it.

52. ETECEN means Empresa Transmisora de Energia del Norte and ETESUR, Empresa Transmisora de Energia del Sur.

Case Study 12: Electricity Transmission in Peru (*Continued*)

Regulatory instrument targeting investment uncertainty	Three different regimes coexist: the mechanism of the Law of Electric Concessions (LCE); the system of the BOOT contracts (Build, Operate, Own and Transfer) and the special regimen of concession of ETECEN and ETESUR

Schematic presentation of the different mechanisms of targeting investment

Mechanism's name	*Methodology*	*Study Case*
LCE	Annual VNR calculated for four years. Efficient Opex	Aguaytía
BOOT Contracts	Winning bid is annualized = annual VNR (this annual amount is indexed by the US's Wholesale Price Index). Efficient Opex. The contract is fixed in US dollars	Mantaro-Socabaya line.
ETECEN/ETESUR privatization	Warranted annual revenue fixed in US$58.638 millions for 30 years.	ETECEN/ETESUR
Form of regulatory regime	*The Legal (LCE) mechanism:*	

The distribution sector is regulated by the efficient firm (tariffs revisions are made every four years). In transmission, the generators connected to the principal transmission system pay monthly compensation to cover the Annual Total Cost of Transmission (CTA).[53] The CTA is determined by using efficiency approaches based in technical and economic standards that take in consideration the actual configuration of the transmission system. The real costs are "compared" with the performance of an efficient firm that supply the same service and complies with the quality and security standards specified by the regulation. Once the CTA is defined, it is compensated through two concepts: the Tariff Revenue and Connection toll.[54,55]

(*Continued*)

---

53. It is the sum of the annuity of investment and the standard costs of operation and maintenance of the Economic Adapted System. The annuity of investment is calculated over the base of the New Replacement Value (VNR) as the costs of the renovation of the installations used to supply the same service, with the current technology and prices, over a period of 30 years and a actualization rate of 12%). The concessionaries present their VNR, but GART-OSINERG has the faculty to reject any asset considered unnecessary. According with the traditional methodology used by OSINERG, the valuation of the transmission installations is made over standard modules of transmission lines with their own cells of transmission, designed to operate in the same geographic conditions and altitudes over which assets are constructed. These modules are conformed by current technological elements and valued by average market prices. Every four years OSINERG proceed to calculate the VNR of transmission installations with the information presented by the concessionaries.

54. The Tariff Revenue is calculated taking into consideration the capacity and energy injected and withdrawn at the bar (valued by its own node price for generation without including the respective toll). This is based on a simulation of the dispatch at minimum cost that allows obtaining the energy and capacity of the system. The tariff revenue is paid monthly by the generator proportionally to its capacity sold. The connection toll is the difference between the Total Cost of Transmission and the revenue tariff. GART-OSINERG fixes the connection toll monthly and the tolls are paid by the generators from their contracts. In these contracts a unit toll, on a per KW/month basis, is set on the basis of the total amount of the toll and the maximum expected demand.

55. In the case of secondary lines, where it is possible to identify the users, two methods are used to calculate the toll, depending if the lines are been used by a generator or by the distributors.

Case Study 12: Electricity Transmission in Peru (*Continued*)

Regulatory instrument targeting investment uncertainty	Three different regimes coexist: the mechanism of the Law of Electric Concessions (LCE); the system of the BOOT contracts (Build, Operate, Own and Transfer) and the special regimen of concession of ETECEN and ETESUR

The BOOT contracts system

A BOOT contract is a contract to Build, Operate, Own and Transfer (to the government). Usually they have a term of 30 years. The concessionary that wins the auction will own the asset of the concession. At the end of the concession the concessionary will have to give back the ownership of assets to the government.[56] Although the *BOOTs contracts tariff regime* is very similar to the mechanism of LCE, the most important feature is that concessionaires have the guarantee—by contract—that they will recover the amount of the bid made in the auction.[57] The recognized VNR reflects the investment of the concessionary considering the winner's bid. The winner's offer is annualized considering a 30 year period establishing the VNR annuity of installations.[58] Opex is calculated by the usual mechanisms used by OSINERG to find the efficient standards corresponding to the notion of the "adapted economic system." Finally, the concessionaire is compensated for the variation of the exchange rate (receives revenues in local currency, but BOOTs contracts are fixed in American dollars). The Tariff Revenue and the transmission toll are calculated in the same way as in the LCE (taking in consideration that revenues over the 30 years cannot exceed the winner's bid).

The special regime of ETECEN and ESEUR concession

ETECEN and ESEUR were privatized on September 2002.[59] The international auction was won by the Sociedad Concesionaria Red de Energia del Peru, whose principal shareholder is Interconexion Electrica S.A. (ISA)—a public firm from Colombia. The concession has a term of 30 years. The principal characteristic of the concession contract is the guarantee that the winner will obtain a Warranted Annual

---

56. Other important characteristics are:
   (1) The concessionaire promises to guarantee quality, efficiency and continuity of the service (penalties and compensation payments are also incorporated in these contracts).
   (2) Concessionaires have to allow open access to other operators and to the generators.
   (3) A fixed discount rate of 12% is used.

57. The BOOT contracts require the government to guarantee the recovery of the investment by the auction winner. In order to do this, the calculation of the remuneration for the use of the secondary lines, obligates the regulator to update the projected variables (demand, etc.) and readjust the revenue of the firms.

58. The VNR is adjusted every four years by the US's Wholesale Price Index.

59. The relative importance of ETECEN and ETESUR in the system can be established by analyzing their market shares. In 2001 the market share of ETECEN (still state-owned at that time) was 55% (revenues of US$59.821m); ETESUR 7.4% (US$8.075m); Eteselva 4.4% (US$4.748m); Redesur 8.5% (US$9.287m); and Transmantaro 24.7% (US$26.846m).

Case Study 12: Electricity Transmission in Peru (*Continued*)

Regulatory instrument targeting investment uncertainty	Three different regimes coexist: the mechanism of the Law of Electric Concessions (LCE); the system of the BOOT contracts (Build, Operate, Own and Transfer) and the special regimen of concession of ETECEN and ETESUR
	Remuneration (RAG) of US$58.638 million for the 30 years. The concessionaire has to supply the service while complying with quality and service security standards, accomplish the maintenance, repair and modernize the electric infrastructure. Investment is limited to the construction of certain established lines necessary for the expansion of the grid (interconnection with Ecuador through the construction of the Zorritos-Zarumilla line). The winner was the one who offered the highest price. ISA bid US$261 millions (the starting price was US$250m)—ISA was the only firm that bid. Clearly, this mechanism is different from the fundamental efficiency criteria of tariff determination established in the LCE. The regulatory function is limited to actualize the RAGs amounts and to distribute the compensations among generators and distributors.
Time frame of case study and the regulatory process	*The LCE regime: The case of Aguaytía.* *Time frame of the case study.* In 1998 the Aguaytia firm finalized an integral project of gas and electricity in the fields of the local area of Aguaytía.[60] A transmission line of 220 KV and 392 km was one part of the project. This line connected Aguaytia region with the Interconnected System.[61] Initially, Aguaytia expected to supply its service to a particular client, but this failed and the firm was forced to sell in the spot market. *Regulatory Process.* The importance of this study case is that it shows various problems that could appear when investments are made under the LCE system (and when more than one regime coexists). The relation between Aguaytia and the regulator is marked by numerous conflicts: on the calculation of the transmission toll in the meshed-grid; in 2000, on the re-categorization of the lines (the regulator, finally, recognized them as, principal lines); and last, in 2001, on the recognition of costs. In this last case, Aguaytia asked the regulator the recognition of the costs of its transmission line based on global costs provided by its contractor ABB (which were justified by consultants' reports). OSINERG denied Aguaytia requests[62]. In this conflict, Aguaytia asked

(Continued)

---

60. The project implied the construction of a thermo-electric gas-fired simple cycle plant (160 MW); a transmission line of 220 KV through "Los Andes" which would connect Aguaytia to the Interconnection System (400 km).

61. Originally, it was considered a secondary line, later in 2000, with the introduction of a new generator, OSINERG reconsidered and defined it as a principal line.

62. GART-OSINERG has power to deny the recognition of any investments if they are found not efficient (this is what happened in the case of Aguatía).

Case Study 12: Electricity Transmission in Peru (*Continued*)

Regulatory instrument targeting investment uncertainty	**Three different regimes coexist: the mechanism of the Law of Electric Concessions (LCE); the system of the BOOT contracts (Build, Operate, Own and Transfer) and the special regimen of concession of ETECEN and ETESUR**
	the recognition of a VNR of US$31,068,276, but the CTE only recognized a VNR of US$19,596,000. Aguaytía argued that the methodology used by OSINERG was discriminatory because in other investments projects, by definition, investments are automatically recognized (referring to BOOT contracts and ETECEN/ETESUR privatization).
	BOOTs contracts mechanism: The case of the Mantaro-Socobaya line
	Time frame of the case study. In 1996 the government decided to unify the SINC (Sistema Interconectado Centro Norte) and the SISUR (Sistema Interconectado Sur) with a line called "Mantaro-Socobaya."[63] The government called for an international public auction in January 1998. The winner was the Consorcio Transmantaro S.A.[64] The line started commercial operations on October 2000.
	The regulatory process: The winner's bid (Consorcio Trans-mataro S.A.) was of US$179.179 millions.[65] For example between October 2000 and February 2001 the recognized CTA was of US$10,842,704.
Rationale for using the approach	Peruvian government thought that the BOOT's mechanism would attract the interests of private investments (more than the LCE system) moreover considering that investment projects are considerably important-. A similar motivation justifies the regime used for the privatization of ETECEN and ETESUR.
Scope of mechanism	
Symmetry of mechanism	
Evidence of performance	
Primary information sources	LCE; Reglamento de la Ley de Concesiones Eléctricas; "La problemática de la Actividad de Transmisión de Energía en el Perú," Ricardo de la Cruz Sandoval y Raúl García Carpio, 2003; Contrato BOOT de línea Mantaro-Socobaya;

---

63. Although the Energy Tariffs Commission (today the GART-OSINERG) made a cost-benefit analysis of the convenience of the line, the project was discretionally determined by the government (there were no market forces to guide what would had to be done).

64. In 1999 the government called for another international public auction to strengthen the SISUR. As in the case of the Mantaro-Socobaya line, here also a BOOT regime was applied (the first project is the focus, however, because it was much bigger than the SISUR reinforcement). The auction was won by Red Electrica de España S.A. and the first phase was finished on October 2000 (while the second one, on February 2001).

65. For the reinforcement of ETESUR, the winner consortium (Red Electrica de España) bid US$74.48 millions.

Case Study 13: Water and Sewerage Industry in Scotland

Regulatory instrument targeting investment uncertainty	Scottish water regulatory system and BOTs
Industry concerned	Scottish Water—the sole supplier of water and sewerage services in Scotland
Ownership structure	There is one publicly owned supplier of water and sewerage services for Scotland—Scottish Water.
	Scottish Water comprises the three former water authorities that were merged in April 2002. The reasons for the merger were to take account of claimed economies of scale but also to smooth out differential tariff increases across a larger customer base.
	Scottish Water contracts out significant elements of its capital expenditure programme. Some of this was done (in the past) under UK Public Private Partnership (PPP) arrangements for a number of BOT type schemes for waste water treatment. There are nine PPP contracts presently in place.
	Scottish Water Solutions was established in April 2002 for the purpose of delivering a large proportion (around 70%) of Scottish Water's £1.8billion capital investment program.
	Scottish Water Solutions was established as a joint venture limited company within a publicly owned organization, 51% owned by Scottish Water and 49% split equally between two consortia: Stirling Water (comprising Thames Water and engineering/ construction firms KBR, Alfred McAlpine and MJ Gleeson) and UUGM (United Utilities and building groups Galiford Try and Morgan Est.)
	The rationale for this structure was that a joint venture will eliminate incentives to companies to act in their own self interests. Because of the equity link each part should be working towards the overall performance of the join venture. Half the projects will reportedly be undertaken by equity partners and half will be outsourced to third-part contractors.
	Scottish Water Solutions Ltd is managing a number of major projects throughout Scotland. Examples include:
	▨ Philipshill waste water treatment works, South Lanarkshire: £6m
	▨ Greenock/Gourock/Port Glasgow—Inverclyde: £2m
	▨ Lochaber water treatment works at Salen/Drimnin/Achargill—Highland: £4.4m
	▨ Lochgilphead waste water treatment works—Argyll & Bute: £8m
	▨ Katrine Water Project—West Dunbartonshire: £100m
	It is impossible to say whether Scottish Water Solutions is proving to be effective in fulfilling its remit.
Sector background	Economic regulation for all water and sewerage and water-only companies has been the responsibility of the Water Industry Commissioner (WIC) since 2000. The WIC's role with

Case Study 13: Water and Sewerage Industry in Scotland (*Continued*)

Regulatory instrument targeting investment uncertainty	Scottish water regulatory system and BOTs
	respect to tariff levels is however advisory to the Minister for Environment and Rural Development for Scotland.
	The forthcoming Water Services (Scotland) Bill is likely to include provisions to improve the transparency, accountability and robustness of the economic regulation to which Scottish Water is subject through *inter alia*:
	▓ The replacement of the Commissioner with a Commission.
	▓ Determination powers for the Commission in relation to tariffs.
	▓ Greater clarity over the review periods for price reviews.
	Investment has been a major issue for Scottish Water and the former Authorities with the need to implement EU directives such as the Urban Wastewater Treatment Directive. The WIC estimates that £1,800m needs to be invested in the four years to 2005–06.
Form of regulatory regime	A strategic review of charges was completed in October 2001 for the four year period 2002–03 to 2005–06 (*Quality and Standards II*).
	A new strategic review of charges is about to begin in the summer of 2004 (announced by Scottish Minister for Environment and Rural Development) on 26th May 2004. This is likely to put in place more formal regulatory rules which are largely not in place at present.
	The system of regulation applied is a revenue cap.
	There is no defined time period for reviews at present which are subject to the decision of the Scottish Executive.
Time frame of case study	The time frame of this case study is 2002 to 2006, *i.e.* the price review covering this period.
Rationale for using the approach	The main objective of the regulation of Scottish Water is to compel it to invest significant amounts to achieve the required outputs (*e.g.* under EU Directives) while at the same time investing in an efficient way (*i.e.* without unnecessary cost) and achieving improved operational efficiency.
	Much comparison is undertaken with the privatized water companies in England and Wales and there is a desire to see levels of efficiency achieved "south of the border".
Scope of mechanism	The WIC regulates all capital expenditure (*i.e.* including expenditure related to base service levels, new quality expenditure and expenditure to improve services and balance supply and demand).
	Investment undertaken under PPP is, however, assessed separately (as operating costs arising out of the contracts).
Regulatory process	The outcome from the price review was the subject of consultation on methodology with the WIC ultimately deciding on its preferred approach.

Case Study 13: Water and Sewerage Industry in Scotland (*Continued*)

Regulatory instrument targeting investment uncertainty	Scottish water regulatory system and BOTs
	Where Scottish Water wishes to make changes to the capital program it does this in conjunction with the WIC, but there is a lack of formal regulatory processes or rules (like logging up/down in England and Wales).
Symmetry of mechanism	The mechanisms applied by the WIC are symmetrical as no consideration has been given to "over" or "under" spends and there are no formal regulatory rules at present (like logging up/down in England and Wales).
	If Scottish Water underspends this means that the Government loans/finance can be less. If it overspends then the Government will need to provide a higher level of finance.
Description of mechanism and regulatory treatment of expenses	The system in operation in Scotland is characterized in contrast to the system in operation in England and Wales, by a lack of formal mechanisms for the handling of capital investment. This may change as the result of the next price review, which is now beginning.
	The WIC makes an allowance in the revenue caps for the capex required by Scottish Water to finance its activities.
	The projected capital costs are the subject of efficiency adjustments using similar methods to those applied by Ofwat *i.e.* standard unit costs supplemented by a good deal of scrutiny of capital efficiencies in other sectors . This has led to the need to deliver a planned capital program of £2.3bn for £1.8bn according to the WIC.
	There are no mechanisms for logging up or rolling mechanisms for a regulatory capital value as in England and Wales. This is likely to be considered for the next review.
	Any capex undertaken through BOT type arrangements (around £550m) under PPP is allowed for as opex (at around £110m per annum). At the 2001 review the water authority estimates of PPP charges were used. There may be scope in the future to challenge these costs and in effect force Scottish Water to try and negotiate better contractual terms. The WIC had no formal involvement in the letting of the BOT contracts under the PPP arrangements.
	There is a so-called "spend to save" mechanism whereby Scottish Water is allowed £200m to spend in order to reduce operating costs. This covers staff severance costs, capital outside the Quality and Services II program (*e.g.* for plant automation) and transforming (*e.g.* customer services and business support).
Degree of cost pass-through	100% of out-turn investment is passed through into revenue caps.
	100% of costs associated with BOT schemes under PPP are passed through operating cost allowances.
Evidence of performance	Recent evidence indicates that Scottish Water is significantly under investing compared to the projections made

(*Continued*)

Case Study 13: Water and Sewerage Industry in Scotland (*Continued*)

Regulatory instrument targeting investment uncertainty	Scottish water regulatory system and BOTs
	by the WIC. For 2002–03 £743m of investment delivered compared to £847 m projected with no more than £600m being spent on *Quality and Standards II* projects.
	The level of acceleration or 'ramp up' required in the investment programme is large and greater than that achieved in the past in Scotland or England and Wales, which calls into question the assumptions being made in terms of the achievability of the projections.
	There is also concern expressed by the WIC that the delivery of capital schemes is at a relatively high cost due to level of inefficiency of Scottish Water (*e.g.* compared to the water companies in England and Wales). WIC calculate that the relative inefficiency compared to water companies in England and Wales has cost around £900m from 1996 to 2003 or £386 for the average household.
Opportunity for gaming	There is little opportunity for gaming although there is a risk that Scottish Water is able to use expenditure allocated for capital expenditure programs to preserve levels of inefficiency in its operations as the incentives are not there for Scottish Water to become efficient.
Primary information sources	Scottish Water, *Annual Return 2002–03.*
	Water Industry Commissioner, *Strategic Review of Charges 2002–2006.*
	Water Industry Commissioner, *Investment and asset management 2002–03.*
	Scottishwatersolutions.co.uk
	MSI, Marketing Research, *The future of the Scottish Water Industry to 2006*, January 2001.

Case Study 14: Electricity in Ukraine

Regulatory instrument targeting investment uncertainty	Ex-post and prudency reviews
Industry concerned	Power distribution sector of the electric power industry
Ownership structure	In total there are about 40 electricity distribution and supply companies in Ukraine, of which 27 are large regional and the rest are smaller local companies. Some of these companies carry out the activity in distribution only, but the majority perform both distribution and supply functions (the licensed territories of the above mentioned 27 companies are respective administrative regions of Ukraine). Both distribution and supply tariffs of these companies are regulated. Smaller power distribution companies are mainly large industrial consumers that own distribution networks and received licenses for electricity distribution and/or supply. Their share in total volume of electricity distributed and supplied is small (except the Ukrenergovughillia state enterprise). They come in both ownership types—private and state-owned. The state of Ukraine owns controlling shares (from 51% to 75%) in 15 large regional power distribution companies and minority shares (from 25% to 30%) in 6 large regional power distribution companies. 8 large power distribution companies are 100% privately owned.
Sector background	In 1994–95 as a result of electric power industry restructuring and unbundling of 8 vertically integrated energy companies, 4 thermal, 1 nuclear and 2 hydro power generation companies as well as 27 regional power distribution companies were created. In addition, the state-owned company "Ukrenergo" (NEC "Ukrenergo") performing electricity transmission via main and interstate networks and energy system dispatch was created and is now the System Operator. All these companies have become the members of the Wholesale Electricity Market ("WEM"), which operates on the basis of the framework agreement signed by all market members. The "single buyer" market model has been introduced in Ukraine. All electricity generation and distribution/supply companies have bilateral agreements with SE "Energymarket". The latter has a bilateral agreement with NEC "Ukrenergo" on electricity transmission via main and interstate networks and energy system dispatch. Large regional electricity distribution companies as owners of power distribution networks have licenses for electricity transmission via local (regional) electricity networks and in addition licenses for electricity supply at regulated tariffs. The industry is regulated by the National Electricity Regulatory Commission (NERC) which was established in 1994. The Ministry of Fuel and Energy still exerts a considerable amount of influence on regulatory decisions made in the sector. The NERC carries out regulation via issuing licenses for different types of activities in the electricity and gas sectors, establishing of obligatory rules and conditions of licensed activities, observing licensees' compliance with

(Continued)

Case Study 14: Electricity in Ukraine (*Continued*)

Regulatory instrument targeting investment uncertainty	Ex-post and prudency reviews
	the license conditions, tariffs setting, development of rules of funds allocation within the WEM, carrying out WEM operations monitoring, imposition of sanctions and fines for breaching rules and conditions of licensed activities in the power industry, regulation of natural monopolies and protection of customers' rights.
Form of regulatory regime	NERC sets tariffs for electricity transmission/distribution via local networks and for electricity supply for regional power distribution companies using a "cost plus" methodology. Each operational and capital cost line item is subject to thorough analysis by the NERC during tariff review. Deviation from the approved amount for each cost category has strong consequences for the licensee: (a) if the licensee under spends on a particular cost line item, during the next tariff review the amount allowed for the mentioned cost line item will equal the actually spent sum, (b) if the licensee over spends, NERC may apply sanctions and completely disallow the balance between the allowed and spent amount from the revenue requirement. The NERC approves all assumptions regarding cost/revenue items submitted by the companies within tariff review procedures. Any additional costs incurred by the companies between tariff reviews are subject to preliminary coordination with the NERC. There is no fixed periodicity for tariff review. Tariff reviews happen mostly on a conditional basis but usually not more often than once in 12 months. The NERC pays particular attention to the following performance indicators of the distribution and supply companies: (a) 100% payment for electricity purchased at the WEM and (b) reduction in technical and commercial electricity losses. Two different regulatory regimes are applied in setting the rate of return on investment for power distribution companies: (1) a fixed rate on the rate base for power distribution companies privatized by strategic investors in 2001 and (2) varying individual rates for other power distribution companies. In the second case determination of the rate of return by the NERC is fully arbitrary. NERC formally establishes a regulatory base for calculation of return on investments for owners of power distribution companies that purchased those companies via privatization tenders in 2001. Those companies will automatically earn a 17% return on the funds spent by the owners to purchase stakes of shares in those companies at privatization tenders until 2008 and 11% until 2013. For those companies 17% return on investments is determined with some adjustments for calculation of the rate of return on debt capital after 2008.
Time frame of case study	1996 until the present
Rationale for using the approach	Ukraine inherited a cost plus methodology of tariff formation and approaches to investment programs' approval as well as approaches to development of the reporting system

Case Study 14: Electricity in Ukraine (*Continued*)

Regulatory instrument targeting investment uncertainty	Ex-post and prudency reviews
	from the former USSR. The process of tariff revision and approaches towards revenue/cost adjustments were initially designed with the help of foreign consultants. The intent was to create a system similar to that of OFGEM in Great Britain. However, in the process of adaptation to Ukrainian specific conditions including political considerations, the regulatory approach became much more informal, less transparent as well as administratively-oriented.
	The NERC adopts its decisions regarding logging up/down the line items of the investment programs based on detailed 5-year investment programs submitted by the companies as part of tariff revision procedure. 5-year investment programs are annually supported by the investment programs covering one-year period. Each quarter and annually the companies submit to the NERC reports similar by design to previously submitted investment programs. These reports specify how much money the company accrued, collected and spend on the implementation of the investment program. Templates for submission of investment programs (5-year and 1-year) and reports on investment programs' progress are unified by the NERC for all companies. NERC has a right to involve external experts when approving investment programs and analyzing their implementation progress, All procurements for implementation of the investment programs must be done on a tender basis. NERC allows depreciation in tariffs in according to the rates and methods of the tax laws. NERC also treats depreciation as one of the sources of financing capital expenses. Any funds spent for purposes not envisaged in the approved investment program as well as in values above or below those envisaged in the approved investment program without NERC's prior consent, are treated as a violation of the regulator's decision and may therefore result in the tariff logging down. The NERC can initiate inspection of the investment program progress triggering tariff logging down at any time. Such approach considerably increases regulatory uncertainty for regional power distribution companies. The NERC also has a right to reject the company's application regarding tariff revision if the company fails to execute provisions of the approved investment program.
Scope of mechanism	All capex. Approaches applied to revenue/cost items' adjustment are identical regardless whether they are capex or opex.
	Revenue/cost items including items of investment programs may be subject to regulatory adjustment in the process of tariff revisions either initiated by the companies or by the NERC. The main peculiarities of the process of revenue/cost items adjustment are as follows:
	▓ there is no specified list of items to be subject to logging up/down. The obligation of the NERC to execute logging

Case Study 14: Electricity in Ukraine (*Continued*)

Regulatory instrument targeting investment uncertainty	Ex-post and prudency reviews
	up/down procedure is not determined formally. The company can apply an adjustment to a particular cost/revenue item only in the process of tariff revision. Thus, application for adjustment of a particular cost/revenue item triggers a full-scale tariff revision procedure rather than a procedure limited to an adjustment of that particular cost/revenue item;
	▓ the materiality threshold amounting to 5% is determined for initiation of a full-scale tariff revision procedure initiated either by a company or by the NERC. There is no materiality thresholds for a particular cost/revenue items. Only aggregated changes are considered;
	▓ triviality test is not applied;
	▓ power distribution companies can apply to the NERC for tariff revision at any time if they suffered financial losses caused by the factors non-controlled by the companies or once output/ costs, either any particular items or aggregated, reached materiality threshold.
	The NERC has scope to penalize companies for the violation of the provisions of the investment programs via exclusion of the funds obtained via tariff for financing investment programs at any time when it proves that such violation took place.
Regulatory process	Tariff revision process is based on the provisions of a formal regulation linked to corresponding provisions of the license conditions. The regulation is supported by a number of other regulations like those on tariff calculation or procurement procedure. The regulation on tariff revision determines (a) circumstances under which power distribution companies could apply for tariff revision, (b) circumstances under which tariff revision could be initiated by the NERC, (c) requirements concerning application documents and procedure and terms of tariff revision. None of the legislation determines procedures like interim determination or logging up/down. The provisions concerning the tariff revision procedure are very general. The procedure envisages negotiation based on submitted application between the companies and the NERC and cannot be viewed as transparent. Almost all application documents are not public and can be accessed neither via request to the NERC, nor via the NERC's web-site.
Symmetry of mechanism	Mechanism is symmetrical, at least in theory.
Description of mechanism and regulatory treatment of expenses	The NERC is entitled to initiate tariff revisions at any time under following circumstances:
	▓ expiry of the term for which the tariff was set. There is no consistency between this term and the term between tariff revisions because there is no formally fixed time determined between consecutive tariff revisions. However, there is a formal requirement for regional power distribution companies to submit tariff

Case Study 14: Electricity in Ukraine (*Continued*)

Regulatory instrument targeting investment uncertainty	Ex-post and prudency reviews
	applications covering the one-year period following a tariff revision; ▨ if the NERC detects any inconsistency between approved tariff and actual tariff in terms of both design and value of cost/revenue items. This also refers to the items of investment programs; ▨ if the NERC detects that material threshold for tariff revision is reached in either output or cost terms. In addition, the NERC is legally entitled to initiate the tariff revision process if it detects that the company submits false information, performs other than licensed activities without obtaining the NERC's consent, fails to complete the program aimed at providing a standard quality of electric power, does not provide full payments for purchased electricity or fails to hold tenders when procuring tangible assets. This list can be amended by the NERC. Non-anticipated capex and opex are treated as if they were incurred during the period immediately after tariff revision. As the companies are entitled to apply for tariff revision at any time upon attainment of a material threshold and the list of relevant items is not determined, the companies have an incentive to apply for tariff revisions as soon as possible after unprecedented or "predictable" changes take place or overstate their expenses in order to create a shadow provision for unpredictable fluctuations. On the other hand there is no officially determined list of cases when the NERC is obliged to perform tariff revision upon the company's request. This enables the NERC to initiate tariff revisions whenever it deems appropriate unless other government entities push it to do otherwise in relation to state-owned power distribution companies.
Degree of cost pass-through	Any additional costs and amounts as well as the ones allowed during tariff revision are subject to investigation. All capital investments are coordinated with the NERC at the stage of tariff revision. Possibility of logging up and passing through of additional investments has to be agreed with NERC. The NERC is not formally obliged to log up additional investments even if they could be put against improvement in the company performance or efficiency.
Evidence of performance	The currently effective tariff regulatory system still requires improvement in order to, lower regulatory uncertainty for the power distribution companies, to improve stimulus for the power distribution companies to manage their cost effectively, provide a fair risk allowance in tariffs and decrease the degree of scrutiny the NERC faces when considering tariff revisions. In practice NERC can be regarded as fulfilling a cost management function for the regulated companies.
Opportunity for gaming	As any application for cost/revenue adjustment triggers a full-scale tariff revision process and there is no certainty

(*Continued*)

Case Study 14: Electricity in Ukraine (*Continued*)

Regulatory instrument targeting investment uncertainty	Ex-post and prudency reviews
	regarding logging up by the NERC of additional cost, the companies tend to overstate their assumed costs and understate an assumed output. For all the companies, except those privatized via the tenders in 2001, the NERC determines the rate of return as a percentage of opex, which is used as a rate base. This is another factor causing power distribution companies to overstate their cost.
Primary information sources	License conditions regarding performance of activities on electricity transmission via local (distribution) networks approved by the NERC's resolution as of June 13, 1996 # 15 with changes and amendments.
	License conditions regarding performance of activities on electricity supply at regulated tariff approved by the NERC's resolution as of June 13, 1996 # 15/1 with changes and amendments.
	Procedure on establishment (for new licensees) or revision of electricity tariffs for licensees on electricity transmission via local (distribution) networks and electricity supply at regulated tariff.

Case Study 15: UK Airport Regulation

Regulatory instrument targeting investment uncertainty	Trigger points (negative)
Industry concerned	Airports—Heathrow and Gatwick
Ownership structure	The major UK airports were privatized in 1986 with the sale of the British Airports Authority (now known as BAA). Only four airports are subject to price regulation—the three main London airports (Heathrow, Gatwick and Stansted—all owned by BAA) and Manchester Airport (owned by a group of local authorities).
Sector background	One of the key issues within the sector is the need to finance large lumpy investments—for example, the cost of Terminal 5 at Heathrow is about equal to 25% of the existing value of BAA. This has led to a focus on investment issues, including pre-payment for new assets through the inclusion of assets in the course of construction in the regulatory asset base. Where assets have long construction periods—such as new terminals—this can mean that consumers start to pay for the asset in a price control period prior to the one in which the asset actually becomes available for operations.
	An issue that affects airport investments possibly more than other regulated infrastructure providers is that of environmental and planning consents. For example, when the price control for the third quinquennium (the name given to the five year price control period) was being established it was expected that Terminal 5 would be given planning consent in 1997 and that construction would begin in 1998 with consequent operation early in the fourth quinquennium. However, delays in the planning consent meant that when the price control for the fourth quinquennium was being developed the dates had to be significantly changed—planning consent was only finally given in 2001 and so construction began in 2002. Operation of Terminal 5 is now expected to begin in 2008—so at the end of this quinquennium and the beginning of the next.
	Again, this concern about the impact of external factors that can have a significant impact on costs has forced the regulator to consider ways of handling this.
Form of regulatory regime	RPI – X applied through a per passenger revenue yield. Basic approach has been followed since 1986.
Time frame of case study	2003/4 to 2007/8—the fourth quinquennium
Rationale for using the approach	Ongoing uncertainty over the actual delivery of investment and the failure of the approach adopted in the previous price control period meant that an alternative approach was needed to protect consumers against further possible delays in investments that were being pre-charged in the price control.
	During the third quinquennium (the previous price control period) BAA had an asymmetric interim determination clause relating to possible delays with the consent and construction of Terminal 5. Rather than utilize this option (something only available to the company, not the regulator)

(Continued)

Case Study 15: UK Airport Regulation (*Continued*)

Regulatory instrument targeting investment uncertainty	Trigger points (negative)
	BAA had made voluntary price reductions in the second half of the period.
	BAA's approach was not felt to provide a full rebate of the pre-payment revenues received during the third quinquennium when this was reviewed at the time of determining the next set of price controls. This led to a discussion of clawback of revenue advancement—something that the Competition Commission has traditionally not advocated owing to the negative incentives it creates (investment may be undertaken even when it is not needed). However, given the significance of the revenue advancement/pre-payment it was felt that some clawback was appropriate—only the second time that this had been advocated in the 20 years of regulatory experience in the UK.
	Not wanting to be put into the same position again, an alternative solution to the pre-payment and investment delay problem was sought. Hence the new, negative, trigger approach. This is a negative trigger inasmuch as the company is penalized for not doing something—*i.e.* it is penalized for failing to deliver the investment. A positive trigger would see the company being allowed greater revenue if it did deliver an investment.
Scope of mechanism	The triggers are linked to very specific aspects of major investments. For Heathrow this relates to elements of Terminal5. At Gatwick it is linked to the completion and opening/operation of the Pier 6 investment project (by 2005/6).
	The five Terminal 5 triggers are:
	▓ Completion of the diversion of the twin rivers in 2004/5;
	▓ Completion of early release stands in 2004/5;
	▓ Handing over of the visual control room to NATS in 2005/6;
	▓ Core terminal building weather-proof in 2006/7; and
	▓ Satellite 1 weather proof in 2006/7.
Regulatory process	Given the simplicity of the trigger approach the process is very straight-forward. A trigger term has been included in the price indexation formula—described below. If the trigger element is not completed then the revenue allowed is reduced.
Symmetry of mechanism	Asymmetric—only applies to the failure to deliver the investment on time.
Description of mechanism and regulatory treatment of expenses	If a trigger is missed, the price-cap is adjusted downwards until the trigger is actually met. The downwards adjustments are:
	▓ Heathrow: 2% for each trigger; and
	▓ Gatwick: 1% for the trigger.

Case Study 15: UK Airport Regulation (*Continued*)

Regulatory instrument targeting investment uncertainty	Trigger points (negative)
	The license conditions relating to pricing for each of the airports have been rewritten. In the case of Heathrow the new pricing condition is:
	$$M_t = \left(1 + \frac{RPI_{t-1} + X - TRIGGER}{100}\right)Y_{t-1} + ATM_t - K_t$$
	Where
	$$TRIGGER_t = DTR_t + ERS_t + VCR_t + CTBWP_t + S1WP_t$$
	The values for each of the elements of TRIGGER are then set out in detail in tables with values for the element being either 0 or 2 depending on whether the element is due and whether it has been delivered.
	A similar, but simpler, equation is provided for Gatwick.
Degree of cost pass-through	Not applicable
Evidence of performance	Not yet known—the first triggers are due in the next year.
Opportunity for gaming	The trigger values, 2% and 1%, are not sufficient to provide a full incentive for the company to deliver the investment on time—the revenue being recovered from passengers through the price control for these investments is greater than the penalty created by the trigger. As such, BAA still has an incentive to delay the investments, especially if demand fails to materialize.
Primary information sources	*Economic Regulation of BAA London Airports (Heathrow, Gatwick and Stansted) 2003–2008 CAA Decision*, CAA, February 2003 (especially annex 9 that provides the price adjustment formulae).
	BAA plc: A report on the economic regulation of the London airports companies (Heathrow Airport Ltd, Gatwick Airport Ltd and Stansted Airport Ltd), Competition Commission, October 2002.

Bibliography

ACCC. 2000. "New investment costs pass-through." Position paper.

Alexander. 1995. *Cost of capital: the application of financial techniques to state aid*. OXERA Press.

———. 2003. "UK Model on Developing and Transitional Economies: Common Issues and Misconceptions" In *The UK Model of Utility Regulation—A 20th anniversary collection to mark the "Littlechild Report"—Retrospect and Prospect*. CRI, University of Bath.

———. Forthcoming. *Cost of capital: A practical guide for infrastructure regulators*.

Alexander and Estache. 1997. "A back-of-the-envelope approach to assess the cost of capital for network regulators." Processed. (Available from: www.geocities.com/ian_alexander_1967)

Alexander and Harris. 2001. "Incentive regulation and multi-year price controls: an application to the regulation of power distribution in India." *International Journal of Regulation and Governance* 1(1).

Alexander and Shugart. 1999. "Risk, volatility and smoothing: Regulatory options for controlling prices." Processed. (available from: www.geocities.com/ian_alexander_1967)

Averch and Johnson. 1962. "Behavior of the firm under regulatory constraint." *American Economic Review* 52.

Bakovic, Tenenbaum, and Woolf. 2003. "Regulation by Contract: A new way to privatize electricity distribution?" Energy and Mining Sector Board Discussion Paper No 7, World Bank.

Burns and Reichmann. 2004. *Regulatory instruments and their effects on investment behavior*. World Bank Policy Research Working Paper 3292, World Bank.

Competition Commission. 2002. *A report on the economic regulation of the London Airports companies (Heathrow Airport Ltd., Gatwick Airport Ltd. and Stansted Airport Ltd.)*.

Concho and McKenzie. 2004. "OFGEM Proposes New Treatment of Capex Overspend." *Energy Regulation Insights* Issue No. 21. NERA.

Domah, Pollitt and Stern. 2002. *Modelling the costs of energy regulation: Evidence of human resource constraints in developing countries*. Cambridge-MIT Working Paper 11, Department of Applied Economics. University of Cambridge.

Fay and Yepes. 2003. *Investing in infrastructure: what is needed from 2000 to 2010?* World Bank.

FERC. 2003. *Proposed pricing policy for efficient operation and expansion of transmission grid*.

Foster and Antmann. 2004. "The regulatory challenge of asset valuation: a case study from the Brazilian electricity distribution sector." Energy and Mining Sector Board Energy Working Notes No. 2. World Bank.

Green and Pardina. 1999. *Resetting Price Controls for Privatized Utilities: A Manual for Regulators*. World Bank Institute.

IEA. 2003. *World Energy Investment Outlook, 2003 Insights*.

IPART. 2001. "Tribunal Guidance on Prudency Test for Capital Expenditure by Electricity Distributors." Letter to CEOs of distribution businesses.

———. 2002. "Review of Capital Expenditure and Operating Expenditure of the NSW Distribution Network Service Providers." Invitation to tender.

Lamech and Saeed. 2003. "What international investors look for when investing in developing countries: Results from a survey of international investors in the power sector." Energy and Mining Sector Board Discussion Paper No. 6. World Bank.

Levy and Spiller. 1997. *Regulations, institutions and commitment: Comparative studies of telecommunications.* Cambridge University Press.

Monopolies and Mergers Commission. 1997. *Northern Ireland Electricity Plc: A report on a reference under Article 15 of the Electricity (Northern Ireland) Order 1992.*

National Audit Office (UK). 2002. *Pipes and wires.*

NEPRA. 2004. *Decision regarding final order on motion for leave for review filed by FESCO.*

PricewaterhouseCoopers. 2003. "Preparation of the Regulatory Regime for the Air Transport Sector: Final Report." Prepared for Department of Civil Aviation, Thailand. Processed.

Sidak and Spulber. 1998. *Deregulatory takings and the regulatory contract: the competitive transformation of network industries in the United States.* Cambridge University Press.

Willet. 2004. "Energy Market Access and Regulation." Speech at Australian Energy & Utility summit, ACCC (available from ACCC website).

Williamson. 2004. "Commitment and adaptability in telecoms regulation." Processed. (available from: www.indepen.co.uk)